Not Just A Dog

Understanding and comfort when your dog dies.

Helping you remember your dog
with more love and less pain.

Pippa Shay

For You

To all those who have ever loved a dog and to all the dogs ever born this book is for you

Contents

With Thanks

Many people have shared their stories with me and, although names and some details have been changed, thank you to every one of you. Through your experiences you will help others know they're not alone.

For my friends and family who have encouraged me along the way huge thanks for all your support and love.

Many thanks to Peter and Caroline at Bespoke Book Covers for their wonderful help.

If a human being could have all the best parts of a dog it's my wonderful partner, Mark. Thank you for lifting me up with love, being my constant cheerleader and believing in this book.

To my dog, Poppy, you truly are why this book is here and will live on forever through these pages and in my heart.

Introduction
First Walk

John sat in the chair in my clinic, trying very hard to hold back tears. He felt ashamed, guilty and confused; overwhelmed with a grief that felt disproportionate to him. It wasn't a person who had died but his dog, Meg, and he didn't understand how her death had hit him so hard. His words came out, whispered shamefully in disbelief, that he hadn't even felt like this when his dad had died.

Just a few weeks before I'd heard a similar confession from a lady called Rose who just couldn't see how she would ever get over losing her beloved Labrador, Samson. Friends had been wonderful at first, they'd all loved Samson too, but months later they assumed she'd got over his death and so she hid her pain. But it still felt fresh and raw.

Meanwhile Mary woke every morning haunted by guilt and the thought that if only she'd noticed Willow going off her food sooner then something more could have been done to save her life. Her death was so awful to bear but the weight of the guilt made it even harder.

Let's Walk Together

If you're reading this now because your dog has died I hope you feel the hearts of so many others, who have mourned the loss of their own friend, are with you now. We grieve with you because we know what it feels like and are so deeply sorry.

This book was inspired by all those I've known or worked with who were lost in grief, not knowing where to turn after their dog died.

My own dog, Poppy, has been my muse and writing companion. Sometimes too she has been a distraction, even an annoyance at times, nudging me to play ball when I'm in the midst of writing. But I love her for those times too because I know, one day, I'll look back and so wish she was still here trying to distract me.

The stories I'll share come from real life but I've made them from a composite of those whose grief I have had the privilege of sharing and helping. All names of people and dogs have been changed to protect identities.

I love dogs. Deeply. I always did like them but it wasn't until the relationship with our dog Poppy began to grow that I truly understood the depths that the connection and love could go.

I've worked as a psychotherapist and grief counsellor for many years and something that I've come across often is the heartbreak and despair after someone's dog has died. Time and again it's seemed to have been made worse because they weren't expecting that level of pain and they can feel embarrassed admitting it to others. "After all", they tell themselves, "he wasn't a human, he was just a dog".

Looking back at having Oliver, our family dog, share my

early childhood, and with our dog, Poppy, playing a huge part in our lives right now I think it's time to get rid of that word "just" and say, with the utmost awe and celebration "He or she was a **Dog**".

The huge downside of living with, and loving, a dog is the sense of loss when they die. I am so truly sorry if you're reading this now because you're mourning a dog who you loved.

You are not alone. At whatever time of day or night you're reading this someone, somewhere, at this very moment is saying goodbye to their dog too. We are connected by the love and the understanding and the loss.

Dogs have lives that are, on the whole, much shorter than ours and a few months to them is the equivalent of years to us. Time seems to speed up from welcoming that tiny puppy to realising you have an elderly dog. We're on different time-lines and so, when they die, even if they've reached their old age, it can feel like their life was way too short. I wish so much that was different and dogs would live as long as we do so we never have to be parted.

Until you've had a connection with a dog it's hard to understand the pain that comes when they're no longer there. Other dog owners will hopefully empathise but it can feel a very lonely place, mourning your friend.

The intensity of the grief can feel a little shameful too as it wasn't a person who had died so surely that loss shouldn't be so bad?

Many people will, with the best intentions, give the advice to get another dog to replace the one you've lost. While that may well help, and many do find themselves in a desperate search for another woolly friend, you can never bring back that unique connection. Every dog is different, every relationship that grows between us has the potential to be so special and, I don't say this lightly, life-changing. But that brings with it the heavy price of grief when that friend has gone.

My hope for you

So many people, every single day, are suddenly facing a life without their dog and a huge number of them are over-whelmed by grief, bewildered by the strength of their feelings and simply have no idea how they'll ever feel truly happy again.

My hope is to help you understand why the connection we have with our dogs is so strong and why losing them so incredibly painful.

I believe I've come across the key, maybe the missing piece, that explains why our bonds are so great with a species that's different to us and why they have such a huge impact on our lives, which in turn makes sense of why we experience the huge grief when that's taken away.

With understanding comes compassion for ourselves and hopefully we can begin to feel a little less lost.

I'll show you ways forward, not to 'get over' the death of your dog but to live more peacefully with having loved and lost your beloved friend.

As you read this book my wish for you is that by under-standing why the connection we have with our dogs is so strong it will make more sense of why the hurt is so deep. You'll be able to find peace with uncomfortable feelings like guilt and regret, feel easier with people who don't under-stand your pain and be able to look to the days ahead, remembering your dog with more love and less pain.

The chapters are called "Walks" and it doesn't matter in which order someone does the Walks as grief is unpredictable. The Walks, just like in life, are different lengths, some brief and some longer.

I've included a Walk on what to do if you're hurting right now and ideas for things to do in your dog's memory.

The understanding of others who have shared the pain you're in will let you know you're not alone with feeling as you do and bring you comfort that you're not wrong or mad or over-reacting. Your grief is not misplaced.

I'll be offering things for you to try that can turn your sadness into tributes, your heartbreak into thanks.

Above all you will gain a deeper understanding of why your friend was not 'just' a dog.

Map Of The Walks

Walk by Walk

I've created 'walks' instead of chapters. Like grief, they don't have to follow any pattern and each walk can stand alone or you can read the book from start to finish. There are no rights or wrongs, just whatever you need right now.

I'm putting the walk "If You're Hurting Right Now" near the beginning of the book. I understand the pain and urgency of finding something that can ease grief quickly so you can keep coming back to this part whenever you need it.

Sometimes you may need to open this book in a moment of desperation to find some comfort just by reading a few words. Other times you might want to share something you've just read with someone else. Maybe it might even help someone who's never loved a dog to get an insight into how it can feel.

Walk One: Making Sense Of Why It Hurts So Much

Bringing together my training as a psychotherapist, the experiences of my clients, family and friends and my own love of dogs I've found what I believe are the missing pieces that make sense of our bonds, and then our pain, with our four-legged friends.

I'll explain how dogs fulfil our basic human emotional needs, why our minds, constantly trying to pattern match, cause us pain, the physical reactions we experience with, and then without, our dogs and why we miss them so much when they're gone.

Walk Two: If You're Hurting Right Now

There may be many times when you just need someone to show you a way forward and to soften the pain. From my experience working with those grieving I'll share many ideas for things that you can do either in this moment or plan to do later to help you feel comforted in your grief.

Walk Three: Saying Goodbye

The time before a dog dies, however brief, I call Pre-grief. Those moments, emerging through the pain that engulfs us, can be a gift to help our dog and that stay with us too after they've gone.

We can't always get to choose whether we're with our friend or not when they die and the anguish of either can remain. I'll gently guide you to make peace with however it happened and to say your goodbyes again now if you need to.

Walk Four: Facing Uncomfortable Things

Grief is so often made worse by other emotions like guilt or regret. When we're able to untangle those feelings and forgive what's needed we can be with our sadness in a purer, more peaceful way. Together we can work through the mess that complicates grief.

Other people can be a great support but sometimes, often with good intentions, they can make us feel wrong for feeling so sad, offer advice that doesn't help or believe it's best just not to mention our loss. Once you have some understandings up your sleeve you can cope with what others say or do in a much less hurtful way.

It can be an uneasy, disloyal feeling to admit there are some things about your dog that you don't actually miss. But you'll see that it proves your connection was even greater than you thought because you loved them despite those things.

Walk Five: Other Griefs

We can feel intense pain, not only when our dog dies but if they go missing or we have to give them away. It's also so difficult hearing about the suffering of a dog you never knew.

~ When Your Dog Goes Missing

Living without knowing where your dog is or what's happened to them can feel like a suspended grief. I'll explain what happens in our bodies and minds when we're in this state and offer suggestions to feel more at peace.

I'll also share ideas of ways to try to find your dog if you don't know what's happened to them.

∼ When You Give Your Dog Away

There are many reasons why people need to re-home their dog and it can bring with it so many difficult feelings. If you're facing that dilemma right now I'll help make it as easy as possible for you, give you ideas for how to help children cope with the parting and share my own childhood story when our family dog was given away.

If it's already happened then I can guide you to a calmer place with that decision.

∼ Grieving For A Dog You Never Knew

When your heart's been opened to dogs it can be very difficult hearing about a tragedy that's befallen one whom you've never even met. Feeling helpless to make a difference when it's too late is hard to cope with.

We'll look at ways to bring some good out of this dog's tragedy.

Walk Six: Helping Others Who Are Grieving

∼ Helping Children Cope

Children often feel helpless after their dog has gone and may not have had the understanding or input with decisions that the adults have.

I'll explain how to make things easier if they're facing a

future without their dog and what to do if the dog is already no longer there.

$\sim$ Helping Dogs Grieve

If you have another dog who's been left behind they may well be missing that member of their pack. Seeing their grieving behaviour can be a painful reminder of your own loss and hard to know what to do to help when you're dealing with your own pain.

I'll talk you through doing some detective work and give you some ideas to try that will help your dog adjust.

Walk Seven: Getting Another Dog

It can be really difficult working out whether to find another dog to fill the hole or to wait. So many feelings can surface from guilt about replacing the dog you've lost to worrying you'll forget about them. Fear can also play a part about how you could ever love another dog as much.

Gently we'll look at these feelings and find the best way forward for you in this moment.

Walk Eight: From This Moment On

When our dogs are no longer with us all that we learnt from them has the chance to continue through us in the years ahead.

You know exactly where you are with a dog, their emotions are so undiluted and laid bare and it's one of the many reasons why connections with them are simpler and easier than with other humans.

~ Dogs Are Our Teachers

And they may well be some of the best teachers we'll ever come across in our lifetimes. When we realise all they've shown us, their lessons have the chance to stay with us always.

Walk Nine: The Love Carries On

A love so pure and strong leaves the shape of it forever in our lives. I'll talk you through how to honour the love as it carries on.

~ Thank You and Never The End

A tribute to our dogs.

Walk Ten: Other Resources

I've gathered together some information that may come in useful to you depending on what you need.

Walk One
Making Sense Of Why It Hurts

The grief that comes when our dogs die may come as a surprise. We probably expected to feel deeply sad but when the pain stays raw and sadness fills the days it's easy to begin to think something is wrong with us or that we'll never feel happy again.

Through my work as a psychotherapist and grief counsellor over the years I've worked with many who are lost in hurt and anguish, not only when a human loved one dies, but when their dog goes too. In fact many people are bewildered, and often ashamed to admit, that they're grieving more for their dog than they did for a human.

It was only a few years ago, when our dog Poppy arrived in our lives as a puppy, that I began to fully understand the expression "Man's Best Friend". I'd thought I'd grasped it before but I'd never really appreciated why it was so.

And then suddenly one day all the pieces came together and it was as if the picture had been staring me in the face for years but I'd been too close to fully see it. It had been hiding in plain sight. Once I saw and understood it the importance of this knowledge and the need to share it became hugely important.

The training that I'd gone through to become a psychotherapist and then the years of owning, loving and understanding a dog began to slot into place together. The most perfect, beautiful jigsaw, one of those "of course" moments, that made me step back in astonishment that I hadn't seen it like this before.

Making sense of why it hurts won't take away the pain of losing your dog but I hope you'll realise quite why that hole is gaping so much and be able to explain to non-dog people why you're so bereft. It will help you feel less hopeless and helpless in the grief and be able to look at whatever is within your own power to fill that hole.

It all starts with something called our Human Givens Emotional Needs. Follow me for a moment into the world of psychology and allow me to explain why I think this is so incredibly important and how I believe it's one of the keys to the incredible connections we have with our dogs.

Meeting Our Basic Emotional Needs

Once you share your life with a dog you realise how people describe them is so very true. They become your loyal companion, best friend, cheer leader, therapist and so much more.

I've worked for many years as a psychotherapist, helping people with all sorts of problems. Because of my training in the Human Givens approach, I always look at whether the client's basic emotional needs are being met. When one or more isn't being fulfilled people can run into difficulties and suffer distress which can show itself as feelings such as anxiety, depression or anger.

The extraordinary realisation struck me recently that dogs, unlike a lot of humans, help us meet every single one of these emotional needs, fully and beautifully. And so this, I believe, is what makes it even harder and more devastating when we lose them. In an instant our emotional needs are no longer being met in the same way.

Think of it like delicious food being available to us, whenever we need it, every single day so we never go hungry. And then suddenly one day that food is taken away and we have to scrabble around, starving, and make do with whatever scraps we can find.

To me this was such a ground-breaking discovery that I had to pick each basic emotional need apart and question if my thinking about this was really true. I kept expecting to stumble and think "Oh well, they meet a few of our needs" but, as much as I tried to deliberately argue with myself, each emotional need was met by our relationships with dogs by a huge resounding yes.

In case you're not familiar with our Human Givens Emotional Needs, here they are. It's important that we have each of these needs met to be emotionally healthy and happy:

~ A Sense of Safety and Security - safe territory and an environment which allows us to develop fully
~ Attention - to give and receive it
~ A Sense of Autonomy and Control - being able to make responsible choices
~ Emotional Intimacy - knowing that one person accepts us completely, faults and all
~ Feeling part of a wider community
~ Privacy - the opportunity to reflect and consolidate experiences, and to calm down if necessary, by removing ourselves from stressors
~ Status - within social groupings
~ Sense of Competence and Achievement
~ Meaning and Purpose - being stretched in what we do and think

I started to look at each need from the angle of our connections with our dogs and this is what I found...

A Sense of Safety and Security

A sense of safety and security can come not just from a dog barking at intruders or delivery drivers but out on walks, when the light fades. Or hearing a noise in the house that, if we were on our own, could be alarming but with a dog there becomes something they go and investigate or we take our cue from them, hardly putting an ear back, and realise it was just the pipes creaking.

We tend to sleep sounder knowing we have our own bodyguard ready to be an early warning system or to lay down their life for ours.

Attention - to give and receive

In a way I need say no more about this because, while I'm sure there are some, I've never known a dog who doesn't thrive on the exchange of attention in some way.

They give us unlimited attention, are the most attentive audience ever, listening and trying to understand every word we say. They don't try and interrupt or turn the conversation to themselves. They want to be with us wherever we go because, if we're heading there, then it must be worth it and they quickly pick up on our moods.

And they need and demand our attention, often at times when we're busy. But their soulful eyes or the hard stare they fix on us makes us break away from that important task we were doing and give a stroke or throw a ball.

Autonomy and Control

The freedom to make your own decisions and be in control, to make responsible choices. This one is a double-edged sword. If it's your own dog then you decide where it sleeps, what it eats, where you go for walks. The downside though is that your level of freedom will most probably become limited once you have a dog as holidays need to be worked around it, how many hours you can be away from home are restricted and spontaneous decisions can become a thing of the past.

But the bigger picture is that you have ultimate responsibility and control over another living being and hopefully use that wisely and kindly. You have their well-being completely in your hands.

If you've had a dog since it was a puppy you'll know that every time it sits or gives a paw is because you've trained it. Its temperament is a lot down to the input you gave it and having a 'polite' dog can give a sense of pride. Even an older dog that you re-home can develop and blossom under your care and you can take the credit and the feeling of control from that.

The obstacles on the downside can be overcome, holidays where dogs are welcome become very appealing, dog walkers are sanity-savers and you decide whether your dog sleeps downstairs or on your bed. And over-coming these obstacles again brings that sense of freedom. You and your dog found a way forward.

Emotional Intimacy

Knowing that one person accepts us completely, faults and all. Swap the word 'person' for 'dog' and you have it in a beautiful nutshell. Dogs couldn't give a stuff if we've brushed our hair, put on weight, lost our job or home, are illiterate or have a doctorate. They truly adore us for the essence of who we are. They want and need us to be, without pretence, who we really are.

Most relationships that we have with people have fragility about them. Even your closest friend can only forgive so much. Long-term relationships can suddenly break down over a few cross words. It would be unusual for a friend not to wonder why you hadn't bothered to take off yesterday's make-up or clean your teeth before going to meet them. A dog sees through all of that and accepts us in whatever state we rock up in.

We can trust them not to breathe a word of the secrets we tell them. They listen, seem to understand and don't question or judge our deepest thoughts. We can be open and vulnerable with them in ways that are more difficult with our human loved ones.

Feeling Part of a Wider Community

Before we got our dog, Poppy, we already knew a lot of people in our village as it's a very friendly place. Immediately we started to take our little puppy out we were met with another level of belonging and were welcomed into a community of like-minded people. These were the kind of people who understood, without a word being said, that when one winter both my partner Mark and I were bizarrely on crutches at the same time for different reasons, we'd need help walking Poppy. We had so many people turning up at the door to offer to walk her that one day, when the fifth person showed up, she was too tired to get off the sofa.

When you're part of a dog community, if you'd like company or to chat or ask advice, it's right there. Even on-line groups of people you've never met are only too willing to laugh and rejoice with you and share your pain and tears when needed. They understand.

Take your dog for a walk and you're more likely to strike up a conversation with strangers. Dogs can be a bridge that bring about human connections for their owners.

Even a smile from a stranger can lift your mood and help you feel less alone.

Dogs too, if they like other dogs around, make their own friends and a walk can become even more fun when they spot their mates across the field.

Privacy - the opportunity to reflect and consolidate experiences

I pondered this one for a while but then I realised that you can have privacy but without the loneliness, if you have a dog around. Even on dog walks, if you need time to think and be by yourself you can time your walks so you're not joined by other humans.

Dogs don't ask questions or repeat things we tell them. You can have a whole dialogue with a dog and know that every word and thought will remain between the two of you. It's a way to talk out loud, work things through without thinking you've lost the plot.

And if you need to remove yourself from stressors to calm down, a dog walk is the perfect excuse to escape and have time alone.

An early sunrise, or time watching the sea, can still be private but made even greater when it's shared with an un-questioning, totally on your side, ally.

Status

"Lord, help me be the person my dog thinks I am". There are many quotes just like that and if you have a dog you'll understand. To them we are God and I don't believe it's just because they're dependant on us for everything. In their eyes we can do no wrong. Maybe their purpose in life is to try and be like us.

But how powerful is it when another living soul holds us up to be the best thing that ever existed? If you need your status lifting then spend time with your dog. Notice the greeting that they give you when you arrive home, your own cheer-leader literally jumping, or trying not to because they're not supposed to, with joy. We are the leaders of their packs and that title carries with it the highest status.

And when you have the best behaved, cutest, friendliest or cleverest dog you'll find yourself walking just a little bit taller.

Sense of Competence and Achievement

That one is debatable if your dog is the one who doesn't come back when called or disgraces you in public. When I was a young child our dog Oliver was very friendly and very untrained which led to a fair few children being knocked over in the park. I remember taking him, with our mum, to a dog training class and, I can't remember why, but after the first class we never went back.

But, when you have the puppy who suddenly becomes toilet trained or masters recall or an older dog who you help through a fear of something, that sense of achievement is awesome. They have learnt from you and, however long it took, you became an expert in your own dog field.

Ever since our Poppy was a puppy she had a huge dislike of our post lady. At the beginning I'd asked the lady if she would give puppy Poppy a treat but, as she was afraid of dogs, she didn't want to. And so the relationship began on shaky ground and just the sight of the post van would set Poppy off barking.

When Poppy was nearly seven a new post lady, Nicola, started on our round and I thought I'd see if you could actually teach an older dog new tricks. So, watching through the window, when we saw Nicola park up the post van I began an over the top excited dance, singing on repeat "It's Mrs Post!" Poppy looked at me puzzled but sensed my excitement as I popped on her lead and out we went to meet Mrs Post. I quickly slipped a dog treat to Nicola so she could ask Poppy to sit and then give it to her. It only took two occasions of us doing this for Poppy, seeing Mrs Post along the street delivering letters, to pull excitedly to go and greet her. No more barking at the post van or lady, a much calmer dog and a big sense of achievement for me.

Meaning and Purpose

This is about being stretched in what we do or think, or finding some reason for existing which is greater than ourselves.

Caring for another being who is totally dependant on you can make you feel important and needed and wanted. There is someone outside of yourself who needs your thoughts and care, who can take you above and beyond who you thought you were.

Your dog running to the door to meet you, the knowledge that there's no getting out of that walk on a cold winter's day, keeping your friend happy and healthy gives life a meaning and purpose beyond your own.

. . .

I'm going to add in another need that is essential for our well-being and met so beautifully by dogs:

The Human Need For Touch

We need touch to thrive. A huge amount of research has gone into understanding our need for touch and how damaging touch deprivation can be. When we stroke or cuddle a dog, even though our dog may not actually be stroking us back, we are still reaping the benefits of that physical contact.

And that wet nose nudging our hand, a paw on our arm, the head resting on our knee all feed and nurture that need.

Even without being consciously aware of it when we have a dog in our lives we touch and are touched many times a day.

When Your Basic Emotional Needs Are Lost In Bereavement

Once your dog has gone your basic emotional needs are suddenly abandoned and unmet. Every single one of them, that you may not have even known were being so easily met, is left hungry or starving.

If you think of those needs as being lost in bereavement too it makes more sense of why we feel so sad. Understanding those feelings can at least help us feel less helpless.

Unless you're going to give another dog a home very soon it's really worth looking to see if there may be other ways you can do something to help those needs, even just in little ways.

I know nothing and no-one can compare with your dog meeting your needs so effortlessly but these are desperate times and some topping up can only help.

These are our basic emotional needs again, and this time with some ideas that other people have found helpful when their dog was no longer there to fulfil them.

I truly understand that each idea may sound insignificant when all you want is your dog back again but would you give some of them a try, on behalf of your friend, just to see how you feel?...

A Sense of Safety and Security -

When you no longer have your personal, furry security guard it's normal to feel more vulnerable -

Walk with a human companion, a group or borrow a friend's dog so you're not suddenly all alone.

Learn some form of self-defence. Apart from making you feel safer it's often helpful to learn a new life-skill, to focus on something you haven't done before, when things have fallen apart.

Set a timer so that lights are turned on to greet you when you arrive home instead of a dark, silent house.

When the comforting, familiar sounds of a dog close by have gone your mind will feel more reassured if there's another noise it can be lulled by. Leave a radio or some gentle music quietly playing downstairs when you go to bed.

Just knowing that someone is out there and aware of your well-being can help you feel more settled. Have a checking-in friend whom you message every day to say you're ok.

Take some time to look at your environment and see if there is something that needs changing to help you feel happier. Sometimes it's something simple like putting a working bulb in a porch light, fixing a creaking floorboard or cutting some branches back so they don't tap on your window in the wind.

Giving and Receiving Attention -

Without that daily giving and receiving of attention it's easy to feel lost and alone -

Let the people in your life who care about you know that you may feel attention deprived and give them ideas of what you need from them. Be specific if you can so they can meet your needs whether it's a phone call once a week or a daily message.

Join a community group, on-line or in person, with people who share the same interests or concerns. Giving and receiving ideas and support or sharing a passion with other people can help you feel you still exist and matter.

Give attention to other animals or people. Notice how

they are or what they need and as you give attention be open to feeling it coming back to you, like a beautiful flow of energy.

Make it a mission, as often as you have the time spare, to find out how someone lonely or vulnerable is and how you can help them. Giving of ourselves to others can top us up too with wellbeing and self-worth.

Volunteer with an animal charity in any way you can, socialising kittens, walking dogs at a nearby shelter or working in an animal charity shop. You're already an expert in the giving and receiving of attention when you do something to make a dog's life better and wonderful feelings can come when you keep that doorway open.

Become as sociable as you feel capable of. When we're grieving the last thing we often feel like is having to interact with other people. Listen closely to yourself and, when it starts to feel possible, begin to say yes to as many things as feel right - invitations, requests, ideas. Take the lead from your dog who probably would have said yes before the sentence was even finished.

Autonomy and Control -

When you lose the responsibility of caring for your dog it can feel like the autonomy and control over your whole life has been rocked -

Your time and energy may well have been focused on looking after another living being and now there's space for that light to be shone on you. Maybe this is the time to see if there are ways you could look after yourself more?

Have a gentle look at your life and see if there's something you could take more control of or better choices you could make.

A little decluttering can go a long way to helping you feel you're taking some of your power back. Just throwing out a few things or pairing up your socks can be a beginning and, if you have the energy, spring-clean your home. Having an environment that is tidier or more inviting can help you feel more at peace.

The same goes for emails, deleting those you no longer need or throwing away pens that no longer work is a way of showing yourself you're taking charge of your environment.

These tiny actions can begin to help us feel some level of control again.

When you feel up to it, with the help of someone else if you need it, step back and look with compassion at any ways you have the power to make relationships in your life better too.

Emotional Intimacy -

Once you've known how it feels to be accepted completely for who you are, the loss of that can be immense -

Tell someone in your life more often that you love them. It comes so easily to show our affection to our dogs but the people in our lives may well be happily surprised when we offer that love to them.

See if you can be a little more open and vulnerable with how you're feeling with other humans. Give the gift of asking for help. It's an honour to have someone trusting you enough to say "please help me" and it can allow that other person to show their own vulnerability more too.

Ask those close to you to give you more hugs, tell you

how much you matter to them, let you in on their most private thoughts and encourage you to do the same without any judgement.

Something lovely to do, even more so if you live alone, is to give yourself a high five. Motivational speaker Mel Robbins has written a book called "The High 5 Habit" where she encourages you, every morning after brushing your teeth, to look at yourself in the mirror, set an intention for the day and then give that you in the mirror a high five. In lots of ways it's the essence of what our dogs give us "I'm on your side, I believe in you. I love you just the way you are. You can do this."

Feeling Part of a Wider Community -

It can be wonderful belonging to a group of like-minded people so when we lose our dog it can seem like our membership has suddenly been cancelled -

Still go on walks at the usual time if you've got to know other dog walkers. Very often the dogs are off on adventures or playing with each other so it doesn't have to seem like you're the odd one out. Most dog lovers will understand and be more than happy for you to remain part of the dog walking community. They'd probably be very grateful too for the offer of a lie-in if you want to take their dog out instead of them sometimes.

Join a group - it doesn't have to be about dogs. It could be a book club, a campaign group, anything where you're sharing a focus with others and being part of something outside of yourself.

Become a volunteer at a charity. If you're able to find some cause you believe in then good can come from it in many ways and you'll be part of a wider movement and find a sense of belonging again.

Privacy -

When the gift of privacy, but without the loneliness, that we shared with dogs is taken away, very often we're left just with loneliness -

If daily dog walks are no longer there, making time to be alone with your thoughts, if you need that, can sometimes be a challenge. Being open with others, explaining it's nothing personal so they don't feel worried or rejected, is important and set aside the time you need, even if it's ten minutes a day.

Even taking a longer shower, parking round the corner from your house or offering to head out to run errands can give you some precious time by yourself and solitude inside your head.

If you feel the need for privacy but with other people around then spending time reading in a library or sitting at the back of a church service is something to try.

Borrowing someone else's dog to spend time with or walking dogs in rescue shelters can bring back some of the gift of privacy with the company that your own dog gave you.

Status -

With your greatest cheerleader no longer around to lift you up, feeling important in some way to someone or being good at something is vital -

The feeling of status can come from being known as a brilliant friend or parent, the best cake maker in the village, the one always looking out for neighbours or someone who can book a restaurant when speaking in a foreign language. With the possibility of a bit of extra free time now is there something that you could learn or get more proficient at? Something that would make you feel proud of yourself?

It can be hard with humans to recreate the effusive welcome your dog would have given you but even a little bit more of making each other feel important can help a great deal.

This might sound over the top but if you have a partner or family then a lovely thing to do when each of you arrives home or walks into the room is to celebrate them. If you can bring yourselves to genuinely clap or cheer each other that would be so uplifting but even giving each other a hug would be wonderful. At the very least smile and say "I'm so glad you're home".

Raising your status doesn't just have to come from your relationships with other people. If you live alone or your human companions aren't able to provide an uplifting welcome it would be very helpful if you can find ways to do this for yourself.

So often we talk negatively to ourselves and are far unkinder than we would be to others. Listen to how you speak to yourself and experiment with turning up the level of encouragement and gratitude. When you look at yourself in the mirror or you walk in through the door imagine the voice in your head is now that of your dog. What would he or she have said? How about something like "Wow, it's you!" "You're amazing. Best thing ever." "You're gorgeous." "I adore you." Try it for a week and see how you feel.

Sense of Competence and Achievement -

Every time you watched your dog, your protégé, behaving politely hopefully you felt a glow of accomplishment. Now though, without them reminding you how you achieved something, it's important to somehow meet that emotional need -

Remember back to when your dog was a puppy or a newly rescued older dog. There were probably times in the early days when it seemed like they would never be house-trained or stop jumping up at people and you felt like giving up. But then the day came when, under your guidance, they suddenly got it. I know what a sense of achievement that gave me. I was at last no longer a complete disaster as a dog trainer.

Bring back those memories now of how, with time and patience, you succeeded. You showed yourself you were competent and that expertise hasn't gone. You still are just as competent and capable of achievements.

Maybe now could be the time to think about something in your life that you'd like to get better at or something you can learn? It may be about discovering a new skill or pushing yourself in some way to grow taller, not only in the eyes of others, but also in your own.

Meaning and Purpose -

These are emotional needs that I think can feel pretty huge and daunting. When your dog was with you those needs were probably well taken care of but finding yourself without them and wondering what life's all about and what your purpose is can be bewildering -

At times like these little steps of gentleness may be what's needed as you begin to uncover meaning and purpose in your life. Take it a day or a moment at a time, without putting pressure on yourself, knowing that sometimes it's a journey of discovery that needs some space.

Begin to ponder with yourself what matters most to you in your life and the world. If money didn't come into it and you could make something happen, what might it be? If you have supportive people in your life ask them what they think is important to you and where your strengths and talents lie. Maybe, when you ask yourself, you might find that justice is something that really matters. Others may say that they see you being passionate and fighting for what you believe in. So combining the two could open a door into joining a cause you believe in.

Or it may be that, on asking yourself, you feel that love is what it's all about. While others may say that you always make people feel better. So maybe there's some way of focusing your wish for sharing love while lifting the lives of others?

You don't need to think big if that feels too much at the moment. Is there something that you can do more of or less of or differently right now to give you a sense of some meaning or purpose? It could be deciding that your purpose this day is to brighten someone else's day and that may mean just smiling at a stranger or holding a door open for them. Very often we're stretched by looking beyond ourselves and that can bring a greater meaning to our lives and give us feelings of purpose and reward.

Or it might be that you get those needs met by knowing that people care about you and that you really matter.

Letting people know that you need to feel that more at the moment will begin to help you.

Need For Touch -

When our hands are used to reaching out automatically and feeling the contact with another living being that withdrawal of touch can come as a shock. It's so important to find other ways to meet that need -

If you can afford it and enjoy them there can be deep relief from regular professional massages. Or maybe there's someone in your life who knows how to do them for free. Even a shoulder massage from someone can relieve a lot of the tension that we hold there. If you're by yourself then stroking your own palms or shoulders can feel good and releases dopamine and serotonin.

When you're out for a stroll explain to dog walkers that you're missing your dog and, if they have a friendly dog, ask if it would be alright if you stroked them. With just some quick physical contact between you and a dog nourishing feelings will be rekindled.

At animal rehoming centres there will be many little souls in need of some fuss. Any animal that you're able to stroke or cuddle will top up your own need for touch as much as theirs.

Hug people as much as you feel able to and they're happy about it. It's impossible to give a hug without receiving one back and we need physical contact with people or animals to really thrive.

Pattern Matching

It was the first cold day of autumn so Jane grabbed her warm coat from the cupboard. As she put her hands into her pockets to find her gloves she pulled out a half empty packet of dog treats and some poo bags. The pain and loss were there instantly, fresh and raw, waiting in the wings for this moment. She leant her head against the wall, closing her eyes against the tears as her mind ran back to the last day they'd shared together.

When you've lived with a dog there will have been some level of interaction every day that you spent with them. Maybe they nudged you awake with a wet nose or ran to greet you, tail wagging, when you walked in through the door. If you had a dog who liked affection they could well have been on your lap, by your feet or lying beside you on the sofa most evenings.

A walk through the wind and the rain probably had more of a purpose when you had a furry friend by your side. A trip to the supermarket may well have meant dog treats quietly slipping into your trolley.

Balls and toys were left as trip hazards or hidden under the sofa cushions.

A dog bed took up proud residency in a room.

Maybe even a trip to the bathroom was a less private moment with the company of your friend.

Without realising it we get used to sharing our lives with a dog and their presence seeps into so many parts of our existence until one day they're no longer there and the loss hits us over and over again.

We walk through the door and there's no wagging tail to greet us, the room feels bigger with the toys tidied away, our hand, that would have unthinkingly gone to stroke a woolly head, now meets empty space. And their bed is mournfully empty or thrown away.

Throughout our lives our brains learn to unconsciously pattern match. You don't need to work out how to sit down on a chair once you've learnt it or which drawer the cutlery lives in. In the background our minds are forever learning and putting things together and they like doing that. The same thing happens when you open the front door and your dog runs to say hello. If it happens regularly it turns into a pattern match, linking opening the door to being lovingly welcomed. When we walk from one room to another and know that we'll have furry company right behind us, ready to get involved with whatever we're doing, our brain is matching those things together.

Dogs do pattern matching too. They recognise the sound of our car door shutting and it tells them that we're about to walk in through the front door. Their lead being taken off the hook can mean only one thing and a roasted chicken taken out of the oven must surely lead to a few slices coming in their direction.

But when something changes or is suddenly taken away that pattern match is broken but our brain is still looking for the match. It pulls us up sharply when we realise things are different and the loss hits us again. Many times people have told me that, after their dog has died, they catch sight of the empty dog bed, see the lead on the back of the door or discover a ball hidden away and the pain is fresh again.

In very simple terms this is what's going on in our minds, unconsciously, in a split second...

We see the dog bed, our mind goes "That's the dog's bed. Oh no! My dog has gone"

Or we find the poo bag in our coat pocket and, again in a flash, we think "Oh that's handy, I've got that ready for the walk. No!"

Sometimes just knowing why these feelings hit us can help, even a little bit. And we can be ready.

Some people prefer to clear out anything that reminds them of their dog because it's just too painful whilst others hold onto everything.

There are no right or wrong ways and you need to do what feels best for you, in your own time, whatever anyone else says. You can make very gentle changes so that your mind re-adjusts to a new pattern, without feeling disloyal to your dog, or you can have a clean sweep if that's what you need.

Letting Go

If you are going to let their belongings go then it may sound strange but it can really help if for every single thing, from their water bowl to their toys and bed, you hold that thing in your hands, bring it up to your heart and thank it for whatever role it played in your dog's life. And then you peacefully and gently let it go.

For any empty space that is now there it can ease the pain if you put something fresh or beautiful or a happy reminder in its place. So maybe where their bed once was place a big green plant in a pot. Or on the armchair that they made their own and now sits empty put a new cushion, maybe even have one made with a picture of them on it.

When you walk through your front door how about

finding a photograph of them that makes you smile or laugh and have it blown up, framed and put on the wall so that it's the first thing that you see?

If you decide to let everything go and don't want to have reminders of them in any way in case it hurts then know that that's ok too. A dog we've loved lives on in our hearts and is so much more than their belongings left behind..

Keeping Hold

If you need to keep hold of their possessions then I have a feeling that your dog would want you to feel the joy that they did when they used them. A water bowl could become something that a pot of cheerful daffodils now sits in. You could arrange their toys and balls in a box frame and hang it on the wall.

There are many companies that make artwork from paw prints or photographs and a quick search on the internet should bring up some ideas.

When you're not sure whether to keep or let things go, imagine having your dog with you as you ask what you should do with each of their belongings. If they had dog friends nearby maybe your dog would like to gift them their prized toys? Or they might want you to wash their blanket and pop it on your bed at night or give it to a dog charity which is in desperate need of their things.

Physical Reactions

Without being aware of it the times in our lives that we share with dogs bring amazing physical gifts for us. It's worth knowing about some of these because it's another reason why we feel so low after they've gone.

Stroking a dog can decrease the level of the stress hormone cortisol and boost the release of the neurotransmitter serotonin, resulting in lowered blood pressure and heart rate and lifting our moods.

Serotonin is a key hormone that stabilises our mood, bringing feelings of well-being and happiness. It enables brain cells and other nervous system cells to communicate with each other and it also helps with sleeping, eating and digestion. Serotonin is a wonderful, effective, natural anti-depressant.

Being with dogs, stroking and playing with them can lift our levels of dopamine too, which calms and relaxes us.

Stroking a dog lowers blood pressure and dog owners often have lower triglyceride and cholesterol levels than those without.

If you have a dog it's highly likely you'll laugh every day at something that they do and laughing does us so much good. It increases the endorphins that are released by our brains, lifting our moods. It improves our immune system, relieves pain, soothes tension, lowers blood pressure and is a wonderful cardio workout.

Oxytocin, also known as the love hormone, has a positive impact on mood and emotions. It can boost our feelings of love, contentment, security and trust in another being and stroking and cuddling a dog can trigger its release.

Takefumi Kikusui, an animal behaviorist at Azabu

University in Sagamihara, Japan studied what happened to oxytocin levels when dogs and their owners gazed into each other's eyes. [1]

Mutual gazing had a profound effect on both the dogs and their owners. Of the duos that had spent the greatest amount of time looking into each other's eyes, both male and female dogs experienced a 130% rise in oxytocin levels, and both male and female owners a 300% increase.

All of these physical reactions are wonderful but the downside is that when your dog is no longer here, as well as coping with grief, it's like being withdrawn immediately from this range of amazing, natural anti-depressants and mood boosters.

What You Can Do

When we're suddenly thrown into depletion of these physical mood-lifters the last thing we often feel like doing is something which could help us. It can take huge effort just to get out of bed and face the day when we're grieving.

I've put lots of ideas for things to do in the chapter "If You're Hurting Right Now" but here are a couple of things to replenish the physical gifts that have been drained.

Move

Do you remember those cold, grey and rainy days when your dog still needed a walk? You may well have put it off as long as possible but their need grew greater than your reluctance until there was no choice but to grab your coat and head out.

Even if it was a quick trip round the block both you and

your dog may well have felt a sense of satisfaction coming home into the warm and dry. And as you threw your coat off, without realising it, you would have experienced a boost of endorphins which are released when we push ourselves beyond our comfort level and give us a high or a lovely relaxed feeling.

Our dog Poppy has a hard stare, just like Paddington Bear, that she uses when she wants something. And if that doesn't work she does a few quick dance steps backwards and a sort of grunting/moaning sound while continuing to stare. It makes us laugh and always ends up with us doing whatever it is she's asking for.

So how about you set yourself a challenge, even if you don't feel like it? Actually, particularly if you don't feel like it. You're going to get moving, even if it's just for three minutes. If you can get outside into daylight and nature then even better but just pushing yourself to move more than you have been since your dog went will help.

If your dog managed to communicate with you in a similar way to how Poppy does with us then imagine their lovely face looking at you or a wet nose nudging you, encouraging you like they used to when they needed a walk. They won't take no for an answer and will be persistent until you get on your feet. And when you do start moving sense them there with you, tail wagging, best day ever.

Stroking

I know that the one you yearn to stroke isn't here and what I'm about to suggest is literally a substitute just to release some helpful physical reactions. In no way do I believe that stroking something else can take the place of your dog. Your body though will still benefit and I have no doubt that your dog would want that.

Find something, your own arm or hand, a soft toy, the silky edge of a blanket, someone else's dog and stroke it. If you're able to and it feels right then close your eyes and imagine you're stroking your dog again.

Just the act of stroking something will begin to decrease cortisol and release serotonin.

Laughing

Without your dog making you laugh and smile every day your endorphins will probably be in much shorter supply than you're used to. To be honest I find it jarring when someone tells you to smile when you're not in the best mood, let alone grieving.

Many years ago our ancient cat Mrs Pooch had recently died and, as I stood waiting my turn in the supermarket check-out queue, my mind was on her last day and my face obviously reflected that.

When I reached the cashier, who'd spotted my face, she said "Cheer up, it may never happen". Without thinking I said "It already has, my cat just died". She was so shocked she was lost for words and I felt bad for unintentionally making her feel that way.

But when we're in a sad state of mind the last thing we need is someone telling us to cheer up and I'm not going to try and do that to you.

I know your dog would love for you to be happy but that doesn't mean forcing out laughter that you don't feel. Even just a glimmer of a smile at a memory of them or sharing a story about the time they did something ridiculous will help. You'll be literally just allowing a few endorphins to fly free and I think your dog would like that.

Trauma

It's worth touching tenderly on trauma, so that if you're experiencing symptoms you'll know what you're feeling is normal. During a traumatic event someone's emotional response can be so heightened that the memory gets stored in the fight or flight part of the brain, rather than in the long term memory.

It's a survival pattern to help us avoid a similar emergency in the future. But the problem is it means we can have flashbacks and panic attacks and feel like we're living through the trauma again right now.

Anything that reminds us of a terrible thing that happened can put us into a state of high alert and fear. So for someone who lost a dog when they were a certain age can easily develop such a fear of the same thing happening to their other dog when they reach that same age that they can't bear to be apart from them, just in case. Or if their dog died in a specific situation they may find themselves keeping other dogs away from anything that resembles that at all costs.

If, at the time of your dog's passing or the lead up to it, you were in a highly emotional or stressful state your brain's alarm system may well have been triggered.

If you are experiencing any psychological symptoms from a traumatic memory it's well worth seeking help from someone trained in dealing with trauma. I'd recommend looking for solution-focused psychotherapists or those trained by the Human Givens Institute with qualifications in the Rewind Technique or practitioners of Neurolinguistic Programming (NLP), the Havening Technique or Emotional Freedom Technique (EFT).

It's extremely important that, with calmness and disassociation, the memories can be reprocessed safely but without you reliving the trauma.

---

1. https://www.science.org/content/article/how-dogs-stole-our-hearts

Walk Two
If You're Hurting Right Now

When Jenny got in touch with me her dog Sidney had died suddenly a couple of months before.

Every morning upon waking she would have a brief second of calm and then reality would hit as she remembered Sidney was gone. Instantly it felt as if her heart was being gripped and the breath squeezed out of her. She had to go to work, facing customers all day, paint on a brave face, pushing the grief down, trying to breathe. She was surprised the pain of losing him was physical as well as emotional and she'd even had a doctor check her heart was ok. She was lost to know what to do.

The day we met at my clinic I invited Jenny to tell me about Sidney and the life they'd shared. She'd adopted him when he was 10 months old after his previous owners moved into a rented flat where he wasn't welcome. His epilepsy didn't appear for a few years and after the initial shock of the first seizure Jenny and the vet managed to help him live a normal, joy-filled life until one day when he just slipped away.

Jenny smiled through her tears as she told me how he'd

been so full of fun, so loyal and far too clever. He'd worked out how to open the fridge door and all of the food cupboards, helping himself to snacks. He needed his tummy tickled before he went to sleep and always found the fun and the goodness in people, wherever they went.

He'd helped Jenny learn to be more open with her own feelings and see joy where she hadn't noticed it before.

So there she now was with this gaping hole in her life and not knowing what to do with the pain.

The first thing we did was to look at her physical feelings of grief. Jenny felt it as a gripping around her heart and her breath being squeezed out of her. She described the gripping feeling like a huge fist, clenching tight.

I reminded her about how brilliant Sidney had been at prising opening fridges and cupboards and how he was exactly the one we needed for this job. Perfect in fact. I asked her to imagine him prising open now, with the greatest ease, not a fridge but that huge fist around her heart and then standing guard ready just in case it started to tighten again. In its place he would put love around and inside her heart and the memories of thousands of days they'd spend together. His relaxed breathing would guide her own as she pictured him there doing his job brilliantly.

I asked Jenny then to close her eyes and allow her breaths out to become longer than her breaths in and imagine Sidney there beside her. In her mind she stroked him, feeling the warmth of his body, the texture of his coat, the way his paw guided her hand to his tummy, where she stroked and tickled him.

I watched Jenny's smile grow as she brought him back to life in her mind and told him how much she loved him and what a clever and good boy he'd been. She told him that the *only thing that was easier now was not having to undo the child locks on the fridge and cupboards any more but he'd been very smart to have made those a necessity. She thanked him for standing guard over her heart now.*

Then we travelled forward in her imagination to the days ahead where she pictured Sidney by her side at work dealing with difficult customers, making their cross faces smile again.

I wondered out loud if there was something that Sidney had taught or shown her that she'd be able to try to do in his memory, some teaching from him that could live on. She sat in stillness for a while and then her face softened "He'd want me to find the best in people, the goodness that's there even when they're having a bad day. To somehow help them to smile again even when they're cross".

How wonderful to take a lesson our dogs have taught us and to let them live on in that way through us.

When I asked Jenny to open her eyes again she was calmer and more at peace. She had some ways forward now to take Sidney with her into her future and to know that he'd be there, ready when she woke in the mornings, to loosen any tightness around her heart and help her breathe again.

There are times when the pain and grief are so immense it can feel like they will never stop. So many different emotions, the loss of hope, the deepest sadness. If you feel like this right now many clients I've worked with have found peace through the ideas I'm going to share. It won't bring your dog back, I so wish it would, but it may ease your pain a little.

Our imaginations are wonderful things and when we

vividly imagine something our body reacts as if it's actually happening. This isn't about pretending that your dog hasn't died but helping you to find some moments of peace within the grief so that you can reconnect with the love that has led you here.

Breathe

Most of the time we're probably not aware of our breathing but it's reflecting how we're feeling. If we're anxious or upset our breaths may well be short and shallow. When we're calm they're slower and longer.

We can also consciously help to change the state we're in with the way we breathe.

When we deliberately take calmer breaths, making the out breath longer than the in breath, signals get sent to our brains that all is well and we can come off alert. This helps to free our rational minds from emotional hijacking.

Do a few calm breaths now - let the out breath be longer than the in breath. So breathe in for the count of seven and out for eleven or in for three and out for five, whatever feels right for your lungs.

As you do so imagine that you're breathing in peacefulness and the connection between you and your dog. With each out breath imagine throwing the pain far away with your best, longest throw ever, and your dog catching it as it flies through the air, turning it into love and bringing it back to you.

Let it out

So often we bottle things up and try to pretend we're ok

when we're not. As the days pass we can feel guilt or shame in the feelings that come with grief, whether it's for a dog or a human. Somehow we believe there should be a time limit on the pain and other people expect us to have got over it. But the more we push our feelings under the deeper they can grow.

Imagine emotions are like someone knocking on your front door. If you try to ignore them or hold the door shut the knocking just gets more intense.

When we calmly open the door and welcome the feelings in they're allowed to be just how they are without gaining momentum from the fight to keep them quiet.

Finding somewhere safe to set emotions free or someone you can be with who won't be worried if the hurt comes out can be very cathartic. Go and shout, cry or scream somewhere where you won't disturb others.

Acknowledge what you're feeling and tell yourself you're allowed to feel that. Add in hope too that some day you will also feel calm, be happy again, but you're absolutely allowed to feel whatever you're feeling right now.

If you need to smash some things up then physically you'll be releasing pent up feelings. Someone you know may be in need of help demolishing something or maybe there's some cardboard that needs stamping on before putting it in the recycling. Even thumping a pillow or a cushion can help. Allowing rage out can stop it building and erupting at inappropriate times.

Feeling the grief physically

Physical pain and discomfort are frequent companions of grief and can be so awful to deal with. We literally "feel" the pain of loss, which can be anything from a sinking feeling to a tightness, a tingling, thinking we're going to be sick, dread in the pits of our stomachs, anxiety high up in our chests. We can feel in anywhere and everywhere and it's horrible.

It's highly possible that the grief is mixed in with being in a state of fight or flight which affect us physiologically as well.

If there are any symptoms that you're concerned about it's always a good idea to have a check-up with your doctor just so you can put your mind at rest.

May I talk you through something to try if you're feeling physically upset right now, just like with my client Jenny?

Notice where in your body the sensation is and what it's like.

Just using this as an example let's imagine you were having a sinking feeling in your stomach, as if all of your hope is falling out of you. Notice what the consistency is like - is it solid like a rock or a gushing as if the plug's been pulled out of the bath? What direction is the feeling going in? Maybe it's heading downwards or churning, fast or slow, or stationary. Is it hot or cold or neutral? Does the feeling have a colour? Spend a few moments watching it.

Once you've observed it you can begin to imagine starting to change it.

So let's suppose it's a gushing feeling going downwards and it has a cold temperature and is grey in colour. Looking at the direction that feeling is travelling in first we need to stop it going downwards so try a few of these things and see which works best -

~ Feel love pulling it upwards so it flows right up and out of the top of your head.

~ Imagine putting a plug in so the force of gravity no longer pulls the feeling down and things can begin to settle.

~ See your beautiful dog catching hold of that feeling as it gushes down and bringing it upwards towards your heart with a wagging tail.

With the cold temperature begin to imagine gently warming it until it feels just right. You could do this by picturing turning the thermostat up, mixing in some warmer air or liquid, or see the heat of the sun on it.

Thinking about the colour of that feeling now, if it's grey then mix in some white or maybe some pink to make it purer, more uplifting or warmer.

Notice how that physical feeling is now. If it's still causing you any discomfort gently play with it in your imagination again until you find a state of more peacefulness.

Invite them to come with you

We've never needed to encourage our dog Poppy to come with us. As soon as she gets the slightest inkling that we're going anywhere she's at the door before us, desperate not to be left behind. Out in the fields, if she's sniffing around and we're walking on, we only need to say "Come on Poppy" and she's with us.

When you're missing your dog imagine inviting them along with you, wherever you're going. Hold the door open for them for a minute or tell them when you're going to bed and say "You coming then?". Each walk you do ask them, in your head or out loud, if they'd like to come too. Every place where you couldn't take your dog before now has an open invitation for them to join you; the restaurant, cinema, your workplace.

Use your imagination to have them as your constant companion wherever you are.

Stroke them in your mind

Close your eyes and bring your dog to mind as they were in full health on the happiest of days. See their face, their eyes meeting yours and their tail wagging. Imagine reaching out to stroke them. Feel their coat, the texture of it, soft or rough, woolly or smooth and feel whether it's warm or cool. Keep stroking them for as long as you need to and tell them how much you miss and love them.

Add in to this you stroking your own arm or palm so you actually feel the sensation of touch.

Have a chat with them

Most dogs love to be chatted to and I'm sure can understand far more than we realise. Often we'll have got used to talking to them as a confidante, sharing our deepest secrets knowing that not a word will be breathed to others. So when they're no longer here the silence can feel thick and painful.

Talk to your dog now, out loud or in your head, as much as you would have done when they were alive. Tell them about your day, your secrets, hopes and fears, dilemmas. Tell them how much they meant to you and always will. Keep on chatting whenever you need to. And listen to see if you can hear what they are communicating back to you.

Tell someone about them

Sharing stories and photos about your dog can help to keep them close by you. If you have friends or family who really loved your dog then keep talking to each other about them. Write down memories and funny mannerisms, keep photos ready to show and tales to tell on the tip of your tongue.

If you don't have a circle around you of fellow grievers of your dog then there are online support groups of dog lovers who will understand the need to share and you can support and listen to them too. Sometimes it can be very freeing to open your heart to people you may never meet.

Face to face counselling has its place too if you can afford it. Knowing that time is yours to speak openly can be a Godsend and if you need to spend that session sharing stories about your dog then do it. A good counsellor will understand why that's important to you.

Thank them

Dogs teach us so much and truly enrich our lives. If we open our hearts to them they can help us become better versions of ourselves. They show us things we might have missed, like the joy on a walk as the sun rises, the delight of racing to see a friend across the field, forgiving instantly, wearing their hearts on their wagging tails. We learn how good it feels to care for another being who is totally dependant on us.

Take a moment and write down all the things that they've taught you and then thank them for each thing.

Then take one of those things and make it your mission that day to try and live like them in that way. It could be a big, unreserved welcome for someone. Being honest with your emotions. Having fun. Not holding grudges. Or being more in the moment.

At the end of the day talk to your dog in your head or out loud and say how well, or not, you think you did. If you think you could have done better just try again the next day. Dogs are our teachers and, even when they're no longer here, their teaching can continue.

Laughter

Completely unintentionally dogs are hilariously funny. And when they die so often does the sound of our own laughter. You may not feel like laughing but see if you can start to allow some smiles back in. Take your mind back to times when your dog made you laugh out loud. Look at funny videos or photos of other dogs. Instagram and Youtube are good sources. No rush but know that your dog would love the sound of your laugh to fill the air again when you feel able.

Walks without your dog

Going on walks without your dog beside you can be so tough. Even finding the motivation to go out can be hard when there isn't another soul urging you to take them.

If the thought of a long walk is putting you off then agree with yourself you'll just go out for thirty seconds. Do that, come home and give yourself praise. Know that your dog would be proud of you.

The next time see if you can make it a minute. Again treat yourself with kindness and the encouragement your cheerleader would have given you.

Once you feel up to longer walks, perhaps on those favourite routes of your friend, take some wild flower seeds to scatter, pine cones to throw in the stream, a tennis ball to hold as you cross the field.

Imagine your dog by your side, so pleased to be out walking again with you.

Going home without your dog

We get so used to walking in through the door with our dogs by our sides or having an ecstatic greeting waiting to welcome us that it can be incredibly painful when we're going in alone or into an empty house.

I've known those who will sit outside in their cars, unable to face that emptiness, until the urgency of needing the bathroom has forced them to go in.

If this is you right now then remember a time when you helped your dog to be brave. Maybe they'd been scared of something and you'd needed to reassure and encourage them.

With our dog, Poppy, for some unknown reason she decided to take against getting into one of our cars although she was fine hopping into another make and model. So we used a combination of pieces of chicken placed in the car to entice her or took a route slightly away from the car and then did a quick U-turn and a run towards it so that she took herself by surprise jumping in.

Another thing that always worked was rain. If it was bucketing down then being in the car was a far better option than getting soaked. Sometimes we need a pull towards or a push away from something.

If you're finding it difficult to go inside your home with

your dog no longer with you or waiting for you then we need a plan. What would your dog do if things were reversed and they were now helping you to be brave?

Imagine them beside you nudging you with their nose or running on ahead and then back to fetch you.

Or see them believing in you and trusting that, however hard something is, you can do it. You're their hero. You showed them how to face their fears and now it's your turn to take a breath, gather your courage and imagine them right by your side as you walk in through your front door.

Giving your love

I really do believe that a big part of grief is all the love that's building up without an outlet and if we can find a welcoming home for it then it can help to ease the pain. If we also receive love back as a result that's even more wonderful.

Most of us need to give and receive love and we thrive when that need is being met. Once you've had that kind of connection with a dog the depths of it can really hit home once it's gone.

We need to send that love somewhere. It doesn't have to be offered to another dog but caring for an animal can provide a good outlet and a sense of purpose. It may be that there's a person or a cause waiting to receive the love you have. As you're reading this someone or something out there is in need of you.

Volunteering can bring loads of benefits and if it's connected with animals then it can be a familiar give and take of love. Many years ago I spent some time at an animal charity socialising kittens, which was such an amazing job. I'd then go round every cage of the older cats and give them some attention too. Just before life got in the way I started helping with the rescue dogs and I'll always remember Dave the dog who accompanied me on my first dog walk there. When the sad day comes and our dog Poppy passes away I may well find myself back there, although this time it will be much harder to not bring Dave and all his friends home with me.

Walking a neighbour's dog, having a friend's dog to stay while they're away, carrying a bag of dog treats wherever you go or even poo bags to pick up after the dogs of strangers can all give an outlet for your love.

If you're not able to give time then donating money or left over dog food and toys can be a huge benefit not only to the ones in need but to you as well.

If you feel ready to open your heart and home to another dog then, apart from adorable puppies, there are so many older dogs waiting patiently to be loved.

But even if you're not ready for any of that, right now in the still of the night or the bustling of the day take a moment of peace. And with your eyes open or closed picture your dog. Then out loud or in your mind say "I love you. I'm loving you right now, so very much, and I always will."

Feelings

When that moment comes and your dog is no longer here, the feelings above all else that I would wish for you would be peacefulness that your dog is now free and well, that you did your best and a deep belief that you will be together again. But it's pretty rare that these are the strongest emotions that people feel, at least in the beginning. What's more normal in these dark days, alongside profound sadness, is one or many more of these feelings and if you're experiencing any of them you're not alone.

Here some of them are so you're prepared if they suddenly arrive to keep you company:

Bringing up past griefs

With the passing of your dog the door to older griefs opens again and tears can take you by surprise as they flow for someone long gone. And if your dog had been your comforter in a time of a previous grief it can bring back the loss of that person or pet as well.

Old grief hitches a ride on this new, raw pain as if it had been waiting for the moment to be freed and seen again.

It's so normal for this to happen and I wonder if often it's because we feel under a time pressure to get over the death of someone we love or the feelings are just so awful we push them under and life carries on over the top. But they're there, waiting and needing to be heard. And when you're on your knees, your heart howling with this new hurt, they find the space that has opened up and emerge, standing alongside and say, "We're here too."

Betrayal

After all the months or years that you shared with your dog, the understanding and trust that grew between you, it can feel like your best friend has simply abandoned you and they've just walked away without a backward glance.

The deeper the connection the more the sense of betrayal that can come. Even though they would have loved nothing more than to have stayed with you it's so easy to feel that if they'd really cared they would still be here.

In the past, if life had been tough, your dog would probably have been one of your greatest comforters so now it can feel like a double betrayal that they're no longer here just when you need them so much.

And however much you'd wished and tried to keep them alive it's so normal to feel that you've betrayed them too, that in some way, if you're tried harder you could have kept them going.

Guilt

When something awful has happened we keep going over it, questioning ourselves, guilt making everything worse. Could we have done something differently, done more, or done less, noticed sooner that something was wrong? Did we let them go too soon, should we have tried other treatments? Or did we keep them with us for too long because we didn't want to say goodbye for our own sakes?

And, however much you loved them and so wish for them to still be here, in a private and secret corner of your heart that you can barely admit to yourself there may even be some sense of relief after your dog has gone - for their sake if they were suffering but also for yourself, after a time of deep worry, sleepless nights or as a full-time carer. But any relief can then bring a huge burden of guilt with it too.

The only good thing that I can see about guilt is the wisdom that may come so we learn what to do or not to do another time. Most of us though feel the heavy weight of guilt when we don't need to. We cast huge rocks at ourselves when we wouldn't do that to someone else in the same position.

Loss of purpose

Every day that you shared with your dog you cared for another being who was totally dependant on you. Even if there was no other good reason to get up in the morning your dog gave you one. They shaped your life with meaning and helped create so many feelings of well-being.

Then suddenly when they've gone it can feel as if one of the main reasons for your existence has disappeared with them and the meaning and purpose have gone missing from your life.

Loneliness

With a dog in your life you have a living soul following you around, a best friend, company, comfort, someone always pleased to see you, interested in whatever you're talking about, never criticising or judging you and it's much harder to feel truly lonely.

When they go they leave behind emptiness and their dog-shaped hole that no-one but you can completely understand.

It can be bewildering and frightening to find loneliness now as your companion and hard to explain to other people if they've never gone through something similar.

Anger

When the pain is deep and so raw we often need to direct those overwhelming feelings to someone or something else. We need to send that anger somewhere, anywhere and we often wrap it and throw it as blame.

The aim of the attack could be the vets, or yourself, your partner, anyone who gave you advice, a person who caused them illness or death or anyone who couldn't help save your friend or who doesn't seem to understand how you're feeling now.

It may be that you feel anger towards your dog - they could have tried harder to have stayed alive or not run into the road or eaten something poisonous.

Sometimes we go even broader and that anger is sent towards God, Fate, Karma or the Universe.

Jealousy

However much we think we love all dogs it can come as a nasty surprise if we feel jealous that someone else's dog is sill alive. Or a loved one isn't going through the anguish that we are.

Life can seem incredibly unfair, particularly if we've looked after our own dog beautifully and someone else with a less caring approach still has their furry friend when we don't.

It can be shocking to find ourselves feeling childlike

emotions and hard to admit them to others, let alone ourselves.

Feeling like a failure

A dog that you've cared for entrusted their life into your hands and with the honour of their complete dependance on you comes a terrible feeling if you believe you let them down in any way. Even if you'd done everything you could to keep them alive and nothing was your fault there can be shame, the feeling that you didn't meet the expectations you'd set yourself, and core beliefs about who you thought you were can be undermined. With that the emergence of past failures push down with their own weight and your very own judge and jury come out to condemn you.

Denial

You may well keep thinking they'll be coming back and simply can't understand that they really have gone. They were such a part of your every day, physically there, on your mind, a big part of the family. When we're so used to having a living being around and sharing so much of our lives it can be incredibly hard to accept they're no longer there.

Our minds are seeking the pattern matches they're so used to making and won't accept or haven't caught up yet with not completing that match.

In many ways too I think our minds are trying to buffer the shock and reality for a while as it's just too much to cope with. So the denial may be a gentler way of easing into the truth of the hole left behind.

Bargaining

We can find ourselves replaying the last moments or days with our dog and, in our imaginations, doing something differently that will bring a happier outcome. We'll make bargains with God, the Universe, anyone, that if we're kinder, nicer, better, do something differently then we'll wake up and it will just have been a bad dream.

We're trying to negotiate to undo the loss and so the grief. When something is so completely out of our control, like the death of our dog, we'll be searching for anything that could possibly reverse what's happened and stop these feelings of helplessness.

These bargaining thoughts can begin to ease off as acceptance of life as it is now begins to sink in.

Feeling judged

Thinking that other people are questioning our decisions or the care we gave our dog can be difficult to deal with. It may be a well-meaning comment from a neighbour saying how spritely our dog looked when they saw them in the days before we had them put to sleep. Or wondering if the vet thought we let them go too soon or kept them going when it wasn't right for them.

We can so quickly feel judged, particularly if we're doubting ourselves. It's easy to believe people are wondering about our decisions when really they're not. And when we start travelling down this path we can think we see more evidence, perceiving questions from others as condemnation, expressions of sympathy as disguised attacks.

And as our minds replay scenarios and we wonder what

others are thinking we can find ourselves, so harshly, judging ourselves.

Depression

Feelings of hopelessness and helplessness carry us mercilessly towards depression. When there's no furry friend to care for or help anymore, when the hope has gone, we can tumble into wondering what the point of anything is and soon we're no longer enjoying or looking forward to the things we used to love.

Everything can feel darker and it can seem impossible that we'll ever feel happy again.

Remember you're not alone feeling this and that, even if you don't believe it yet, someday the light will begin to shine in your life again.

Exhaustion

Don't be surprised if you feel utterly exhausted. It may be that you've had sleepless nights before your dog died with the worry or care for them. And since they've gone your sleep may be broken or filled with dreams and nightmares.

If you do find you're dreaming more then this is your unconscious mind's way of trying to make sense and take action on the thoughts and feelings you've been having by using metaphors that somehow tie into the feelings. There's a brilliant video by psychologist and Co-Founder of the Human Givens approach, Joe Griffin, explaining why we dream and I'll pop the details in the Other Resources section.

Crying is exhausting too and grieving all consuming.

Your mind will be working on processing and trying to make sense of what's happened, while you're awake and asleep.

Desperation

Just like the actual or metaphorical wringing of your hands the feelings of having lost all hope can be so great that you can't see a way forward and have no idea what to do or where to turn. If you're feeling this anguish your emotional brain may well have hijacked your logical, thinking brain and the grief will have overwhelmed you, making it very difficult to think clearly.

When we're in a highly emotional state we can go into fight and flight and also freeze, like a rabbit caught in headlights. We can find ourselves behaving in ways that we may not have before, in urgent, starving need of help.

What To Do

Any one of these emotions can take people by surprise and make a sad situation feel even worse but you really won't be alone if these feelings, or any others, are present.

They can be uncomfortable and bewildering. We may think we shouldn't be feeling that way or find that we don't like that part of ourselves much.

But the more we try and fight emotions or ignore them the more persistent they can become, like a child shouting louder if we're not listening. When we try and suppress an emotion it becomes stronger.

Think about laughing when it's completely inappropriate. The more you know you shouldn't laugh, and you desperately try to withhold it, the more the uncontrollable urge to laugh takes over and the funnier it becomes.

I know this from my own experience. On several, very serious occasions, something funny has happened and it's been almost impossible to hold the laughter back.

But I've learnt that if I find something funny when I really shouldn't be laughing if I say to myself "You can laugh then. Go on" suddenly the joke falls flat. When we give an emotion permission to be present and to be allowed out it doesn't need to build.

So with compassion let whatever feeling is there know you're listening. Tell it you understand and it's allowed to feel like that and you're not surprised. Give it permission to just be.

Imagine opening your front door to the emotion that's there instead of trying to hold it shut while it knocks loudly. With compassion invite it in.

Wrap your arms around it, sit beside it, talk to it. Ask what it needs from you. An obvious answer that may come is that it just wants your dog back. Tell it you do too. And you're so, so sorry that you can't make that happen. Ask what you can do to help ease the feeling. Maybe that part needs to howl, to throw some plates at a wall, to talk about your dog or be reassured you did the right thing or that someday you will be together again.

Sometimes just being listened to, allowed and heard can help and that emotion may begin to calm slightly.

Or, as you listen, you may get a sense of something that you need to do to start feeling more at peace. It could be anything from calling the vets and asking them if you made the right decision, to thinking of ideas that will keep your dog's memory alive.

When something so far removed from what we wanted has happened shifting anything into our control can be helpful.

What could you do now? What's possible? Taking some sort of action will bring a different energy along and maybe a glimmer of hope. So, whether or not you decide to take it any further, look at dog rehoming sites, see what charities are in need of donations, think about whether you could do a walk in memory of your dog to raise money or awareness, go and buy some balls to leave in a park. Make contact with a pet bereavement helpline. Start writing a book about your dog. Find the happiest photos of your dog to frame. Anything. It doesn't really matter what you do if it shows that feeling that you've heard it and you're doing something.

When we're lost we need some sort of direction to begin travelling in, even if we change paths further along the line. Just something to help guide us away from the painful place we're held in now.

Time To Rest

As I'm sitting here writing this our dog Poppy is gently snoozing a few feet away. The years are flying by and she'll be ten this year. I hope with all my heart that we've got many more years ahead with her but realistically I know that may well not be the case. And if I think too much about that then the sadness begins to overwhelm the days that we have now. I know that there will come a time when I'll be picking up this book to read, not as the author but as someone trying to find air to breathe through the grief.

And so I'm having to take time to pause while I'm writing, sometimes for days at a time, because my focus is all about our dogs no longer being with us and, even though mine still is, it can still feel raw and painful.

So it is with grief. When we find ourselves the unwilling partners of this tragic emotion, it can be so all-consuming that every moment is filled with it.

It can also feel that grief is the only thing holding us to the dog we loved. Over the years I've heard from clients many times that they are afraid of letting go of the grief, whether it's for a person or a pet. They fear that once that's gone then they will have moved on and away and will forget. That can feel so painful, so disloyal that, however awful, they will hold tight to the grief as it's the last connection they have.

Many years ago, when I was training to be a psychotherapist, one of my brilliant teachers talked about making time for grieving and doing it properly but not needing to do it all of the time. He likened it to football players or athletes training hard and then needing to rest. If they continue to train for every hour of the day then their muscles don't have time to repair. And it's too important to not do properly.

The same goes for grief. It's too important. The loss of your dog is too huge to not give it your full attention and that's easier to do if it's not spilling into every moment of every day. It's like a vital conversation that needs the full attention of everyone concerned for a contained time and not scattered throughout the day. It can be repeated every day, for as many days as are needed, but in a more contained time.

Imagine you decide every day from say 6-7pm that you are going to think and talk only about your dog. You are going to fully focus on him or her, look at photos, share memories, shed tears, offer up prayers and thanks, whatever you need to do. Nothing, apart from an emergency, is going to interrupt you because this is of great significance. Your dog was and still is so important.

At other times in the day thoughts and feelings about your dog may well show up needing attention, just like that wet nose nudging you. Acknowledge them, they're of great value, and let them know that you will give them your full attention at 6pm. If it helps then have a notebook with you that you can jot thoughts down on so you can really look at them later.

It so doesn't mean that you're not allowed to think about or mourn your dog at others times but just knowing that you have a specific time, if you need it, to really sit with how you're feeling, can be helpful.

As the weeks pass, if you find you don't need that full amount of time or it feels right to space it out over more days that's just fine. This is about you and what you need. And it absolutely doesn't mean you're forgetting your dog, it's just that the rawness of the grief may be passing.

Walk Three
Saying Goodbye

The saddest part of loving any other being is when it's time to say goodbye. And that doesn't get any easier if it's a dog. The love and the connections we make come with this huge price of heartbreak to pay.

Every time I'm faced with the loss of a person or a pet I think how much easier life would be if we never loved anyone or anything as we'd spare ourselves the desperate emotions that come with grief. But then our lives would be empty of all the wonderful things that come with love.

And much as saying goodbye to our dogs is something most of us never want to happen the pain is there as a testament to the richness of the love that we've shared.

As you say goodbye and mourn tell yourself or shout it out loud to the hills that saying goodbye hurts so much because you loved your friend so much and you always will.

The Gift of Pre-Grief

If you're reading this now knowing that the day is coming soon when your dog will leave this life, my heart goes out to you.

Something that you may well be feeling is anticipatory grief or what I call 'Pre-Grief'. A state of foreboding, anxiety, dread, fear, pain, fight, flight or freeze. And the worry that you'll make the right decisions.

Amongst this living nightmare, if you look quietly, you may well find a gift. Even if that time of pre-grief is limited there may be a chance to prepare, to do something to make your dog's last days or moments better, and also to do all that you can to look after yourself and to help you in the coming time to grieve without regret.

Anna knew, after tests and x-rays and honest, tear-filled conversations with the vet that Henry, her nine year old red setter, had probably only a week or so left before they needed to help him on his way. Processing this news at first pushed her into the numbest, darkest place but as the hours began to slip by she knew that she didn't want his final days to be like this for him.

A few times a year they'd always driven to the beach and at the end of a day filled with running in and out of the waves they'd gone to the ice-cream van before heading home. Anna had always been mindful that she'd saved just the last bit of cone for him with a couple of licks of ice-cream as she wasn't sure how good it was for him.

This time she checked the weather forecast and tomorrow down on the coast it looked like a perfect day. She really hoped that, although it was still a bit early in the season, the ice-cream van would be there.

She called the vet to explain what she wanted to do and was reassured that the journey would be fine for him even if their time on the beach may need to be shorter than normal. She packed extra blankets and towels in the car to get him warm and dry afterwards, his favourite snacks and balls and filled the car up with fuel the night before to cut out wasted time on their journey.

The next morning, up early, she asked Henry if he'd like to go to the beach. Immediately he was at the front door and as soon as she opened it, like a magic trick, he was there waiting by the car. Her heart was warmed and she knew she'd made the right decision.

Every moment they spent on the beach that day was more poignant than ever. She was glad of her sunglasses as her laughter and tears were so instantly interchangeable. She took a selfie of the two of them, sitting on a rock in the sunshine, but knew that even without a camera this moment would be etched in her heart forever.

When she felt Henry tiring they made their slow way back up to the carpark and there waiting for them was the ice-cream van. This time all the rules were put aside and instead of just one ice-cream she asked for two. One for her and one for her beautiful friend.

Throughout our dogs' lives they make friendships both with other dogs and with humans. Some dogs have many friends and others feel more comfortable just with their owners. If you have a sociable dog and a bit of time on your side then, if you can, invite one or two people or a dog friend round at a time to spend some moments with your dog. This can become an important part of the pre-grieving time, sharing the love and connections. Hopefully your dog will be lifted seeing people she loves and you will know that you're not alone with loving her and mourning her when she's gone, which can be a huge comfort.

Sometimes we don't have the luxury of time on our sides to make a wonderful last few weeks or even days. If we have any time at all it may literally be a few moments.

Many years ago my grandfather was walking along the road with his spaniel, Josie. She was well trained and, as usual, off the lead. Something must have caught her attention on the other side of the road and she darted across, straight in front of a car. I was too young then to know much about what happened next but I do know my grandfather carried her home in his arms so she must have died instantly or very quickly after being hit.

With times like these there literally might only be a few seconds for a last connection so please forgive yourself for however you react as shock can easily take over. If you're able to then tell your dog you love them, that they're a good boy or girl and thank them for being such a wonderful part of your life. But if you can't think straight or form words then remember that your dog knows and trusts in your love anyway.

As you face this time of pre-grief imagine the arms of so many others, who know just how you feel, around your shoulders.

Try These:

Calmness is key when faced with what's coming so make time to take some calm breaths, letting the out-breath be longer than the in-breath. This will send signals to your brain that you can calm down. And when we're calm we can think more clearly.

As you take a pause, even if you only have a moment, ask yourself these questions and listen to the answers that come:

~ What do you need to tell your dog? Maybe that you'll love them forever, thank them for all they taught you, that you'll be ok.

~ What would you like them to hear? How about "You were the best dog ever", "You're such a good boy/girl", "I love you", "Your work here is done, run free now my friend".

~ Is there anything you can do for them now to help them feel better? Maybe some gentle stroking or a tummy rub, a trip to the beach, inviting their best human or dog friend round, keeping them company, giving them space to sleep undisturbed, giving them their favourite treat, making them warmer or cooler...

~ If there is some time while you have them with you still then ask for second opinions from vets, do your own research to see if anything else can be done. Even if nothing comes of it you will have some reassurance as you look back that you did all that you could.

You know your dog better than anyone and when you

can find the calmness to listen and trust yourself it will be easier to know the right thing to do to help them.

Whether you're in the state of pre-grief now or looking back at that time please send yourself some compassion. It can be such an unreal, nightmarish place to be and it's so normal, with hindsight or in the moment, to wonder if we're getting it right or we could have done better

If you're preparing to say goodbye get a sense of a wonderful Being, waiting in the wings, getting ready to gently take your dog into their loving safekeeping when the time comes, to look after them until you can be together again.

Being With Them When They Die

It hadn't been as Mike and Cathy had hoped. They'd both arranged a few days off work so they could be at home together to spend time with their spaniel, Summer, in her final days. They'd planned for the vet to come to their home on Thursday to put her to sleep and talked about how they'd both stroke her while she lay on the sofa with them and chat quietly as she slipped away.

But by Wednesday afternoon things weren't looking good and the vet advised them to bring her into the surgery. And so it was there that they had to say a rushed goodbye, not in the comfort of their home but the clinical setting of the vets.

For Mike and Cathy this added another layer of grief and uncomfortable regret that they hadn't given Summer the send-off she'd deserved.

For Lisa, the memory of the day she'd tried to save her dog Charlie's life was so powerful it felt like it had happened yesterday and not three years ago. Rationally she knew there was nothing she could have done but somehow that didn't help and the feeling she'd failed her friend stayed with her.

When I imagine the very best way of letting our dogs go it's in their own home with all those they adore around them. It's very peaceful and as beautiful as can be as their soul leaves their body, surrounded by love and thanks for a life so well lived. If this is what you shared with your dog then I'm so grateful that it was that way and I hope the memories of those last moments bring you much comfort.

For many others though the reality is often different to how they'd hoped it would be and that can leave behind feelings of regret, a deep sadness and even trauma.

Many will have tried to have been strong for their dogs but dissolved into tears, others may have been helpless as they tried to save their life.

If your dog didn't slip away peacefully or you feel you could have handled it better in some way please know you're being held in the hearts of many who have gone through something similar.

One of the wonderful things about dogs is how much they live in the moment. They don't look back and think how things could have been better. They're focused here in the now, without the layers of complicated emotions that make our own lives difficult. And I believe they can still help and teach us even after they've gone.

Try this now:

Whatever happened in their final moments, whatever it is that you regret or were traumatised by, imagine your dog arriving to visit you from wherever they are now, fit, well and happy again.

Spend however long you need greeting each other. Maybe you need a good long snuggle together or to sit side by side as you tell each other about all the days since you last met.

As your dog stays with you let them know how much you wish their parting had been different. If you feel you need to then tell them that you're sorry.

Then listen as they let you know that their passing was just one tiny part of a whole lifetime with you. They've only remembered it now because you reminded them and now it will vanish again from their thoughts because what stays is the love and there was, and still is, so much love between you both.

Bring to mind a lovely memory that you shared. It doesn't have to be anything huge, it could be the way they greeted you as you walked in through the front door.

Make the picture of that memory as big as you can, add in colour and movement and sound. Turn up the volume of it and make it as big and bright as you can.

And then take the old, traumatic or sad memory of their passing and begin to make it smaller. Take out the colour and sound and movement. Shrink it down until you can barely see it so you know it happened but it was just a tiny part in the whole of their life with you.

Imagine your dog staying around you or coming and visiting every now and then and reminding you there's no need to hold onto anything painful now. The love you shared is what matters and that will stay with you forever.

Not Being With Them When They Die

"He was my best friend and I really tried but I just couldn't bear to be with him when he needed me, when it really mattered"

Peter kept focusing on his hands resting together in his lap as he told me about his dog Murphy. They'd been inseparable and he'd promised him he'd be there with him until the end. But at the vets that day, when it was time to put him to sleep, his emotions were just too strong for him to bear. He'd had to say goodbye to Murphy in the consulting room and leave his wife there by his side while he waited in the car. He'd just held himself together enough to stroke him and thank him for being such a loyal friend and tell him he'd be back in a minute as he walked out of the room and to the car before his tears began to fall.

He'd never been very good, he told me, at knowing how to handle difficult emotions but he couldn't get it out of his head that he'd abandoned Murphy right at the end.

We talked about the relationship that they'd had and how in-tune they'd been together, how deep their trust was in the other.

I asked him, if he had managed to stay with Murphy, what might have happened? Peter was quiet for a moment and then whispered that he may well have tried to stop the vet just before the injection went in or have started bawling his eyes out as he watched his friend slipping away.

I wondered out loud to Peter if it had then perhaps been a final gift to Murphy that he hadn't stayed by his side? That his dog's last connection was hearing that his best friend would be back in a minute? And that he'd gone to sleep peacefully knowing all was well? There had been nothing to fear, no *anguish for Murphy to witness and his trust in Peter meant he would see him again in a minute and could just let himself fall into this blissful sleep first that was gently embracing him.*

As Peter's eyes looked into mine I told him that the pain he himself had been bearing was because of the gift he'd given his friend by sparing him from worry and distress. That maybe Peter had done the kindest thing without realising it at the time and Murphy had passed peacefully knowing he was loved and Peter would return very soon and then they'd carry on with their day, side by side, as normal.

Meanwhile, two counties away, Harriet got the frantic call from her boyfriend Paul to tell her their dog Mizzie had just been hit by a car and killed instantly. She'd chased a pheasant across two fields and out onto the main road, oblivious to the shouts from Paul, all recall forgotten, her mind on the pheasant and nothing else.

By the time Harriet reached home Mizzie looked like she was just asleep on her blanket in the garden. She expected her to raise her head and spring into an excited greeting but as Harriet knelt down beside her and gently stroked her face Mizzie didn't move.

When I came to work with Harriet a little while later she was still so bereft that she hadn't been with her crazy little friend in her last moments, hadn't told her she loved her or held her as her spirit left her body. Because she hadn't seen Mizzie die she still couldn't quite accept that she was gone.

I asked her how much fun Mizzie would have been having chasing that pheasant and Harriet smiled as she described how her dog literally seemed to exude happiness when she was running after something and nothing else mattered. She was in a state of pure ecstasy.

We talked about how we never want our dogs to die but if she could have chosen a way for Mizzie to go might it have been when she was in this wonderful state of happiness, with no illness or slowing down for such a spritely dog? Through her tears Harriet nodded "And I think that's the way Mizzie would have wanted it."

But we were still left with Harriet not having been with Mizzie or holding her as she died or telling her she loved her. So, with Harriet's agreement, we decided to re-write that scene, not to prevent Mizzie's death but to make it easier for Harriet.

I asked her to close her eyes and imagine watching that scene from a distance and that this time she was back there with Mizzie, running alongside her across the fields, chasing the pheasant together, the wind on their faces, glancing at each other as they shared this wonderful, delightful adventure.

Harriet kept calling out to Mizzie that she loved her, always had and forever would. And Mizzie's eyes told Harriet the same. The love was intense and alive between them, sharing this crazy adventure, as they reached the road and the car took Mizzie's life in an instant.

Harriet, with eyes still closed, imagined seeing herself cradling her little dog and wrapping her in love for her onward journey as she saw people and animals she'd loved before, long gone, waiting to take Mizzie, to love her and run with her too. With a last kiss on her beautiful dog's face she handed her over to their safe keeping.

When Harriet opened her eyes there was calmness now around her. We looked to the days ahead and she mentioned how she now felt like going back to running again and when she did she'd imagine Mizzie whizzing along beside her as her inspiration. Never forgotten, always with her but in a happier way.

―――――

Early one morning Rachel had woken to check on her ageing Labrador Ronnie and found him, paw tucked around his teddy, peacefully passed away in his bed a few feet away.

She had adjusted her life around him over the last few months to make sure he was never alone, that she would be by his side when the time came for his last breath, this amazing dog who had always been by her side, supporting her when she'd needed it.

And now he had gone with just his teddy as a comfort while she'd slept deeply for once in her bed. The thought that she'd betrayed him was haunting her but almost worse was the feeling that he had left without letting her know or waiting to say goodbye.

Rachel told me how, since he'd been a puppy, he'd been a constant in her life through redundancies, divorce, the death of her parents and a move halfway across the Country to start a new life. He'd always known what she'd needed, whether it was sitting peacefully by her side or playing the clown to make her laugh. It was as if his main purpose in life had been to make her happy and show her life would somehow get better.

I asked her, apart obviously from losing Ronnie, how her life was now. With a sad smile she described a new love that had started to blossom a few weeks before Ronnie had died and how she'd told her dear dog all about him and then they'd met a couple of times. Ronnie had taken to him instantly and showed relief rather than any jealousy that Rachel now had someone else special in her life. She felt as if Ronnie had given her his blessing.

But even with this new love in her life the sadness and her feeling of betrayal were pulling her down.

I asked her about Ronnie's bed and what it had been like. She laughed as she said she'd accidentally ordered the wrong size some years before so it was massive but Ronnie had loved it so much the bed had stayed even though it had taken up most of her bedroom floor.

When she'd been lying in her own bed he was still close enough for them to keep a watch over each other as they slept. There had been enough room in his bed for her too and many times in the past she had lain down beside him for a quick cuddle.

So she closed her eyes as I spoke about our dogs and the roles they play and the jobs they do so well. And how Ronnie had been her guardian for many years, looking after her as much as she'd looked after him. How he'd kept going and loved being responsible for her, even though he was old and tired, until he knew there was someone else who would take over that role. How much of a relief that must have been for him and how, when he'd looked over at Rachel sleeping so soundly in her bed, he knew his work was done.

I asked Rachel to imagine gently lying down beside him in his bed for his final hours, wrapping her arms around him and his teddy, thanking him for being there for her and for all he'd given her.

I asked her how it would be to quietly tell him that, because of his love, she would be fine now and that there was someone else ready to take on his job. That with all her heart she loved him and it was time now for him to let go. To run

free of his tired body and that one day they'd be together again.
With her eyes closed she nodded and I watched as her tears
fell and washed away the betrayal she'd felt and with the
deepest love and thanks she let Ronnie go.

———

When we don't have the chance to say goodbye it can feel as
if something hugely vital is left undone. There can be colli-
sions of feelings from guilt to anger, disbelief to shock and
many others in between.

If you weren't there when your dog died it can be very
helpful to prepare that younger you back there for what's
about to happen and to find ways to say goodbye, to bring you
some comfort and peace. Even though we can't bring them
back again the connection and love we had with our dogs
remains.

Try this:

Our imaginations are powerful resources that can help us
and here is something to try by yourself or with someone to
guide you.

If you're alone then have a read of this first so you can
then close your eyes and take your time to go through the
steps in your mind. If someone else is with you ask them to
read these out slowly, a step at a time, so you can allow your
imagination to take you on a journey.

Step 1 - When you feel ready and you have some time for
yourself find a quiet place where it's safe for you to close
your eyes.

Step 2 - Allow your breathing to be calm, letting the out-breath be longer than the in-breath. Imagine breathing in for the count of 7 and out for the count of 11 for several breaths. Imagine breathing in the love and the presence of your dog there to help you. And with each breath out get a sense of the hurt and pain leaving.

Step 3 - Stroke your palms to release serotonin.

Step 4 - Get a sense of your dog now, fully restored to health, by your side, letting you know they're fine now and explaining to you what was about to happen back there. They want you to be prepared, to take some of the shock away, and tell you that their passing was just one moment in their whole life with you and, even though you weren't there, they felt your love all around them.

Step 5 - Keep stroking your palms and let your dog know that you would have given anything in the world to have kept them with you.

Step 6 - Imagine the scene from far, far away, so you can only just make it out, of your dog in his or her final moments but this time picture yourself there too, right there beside them, helping them, comforting them in whatever way they need. Maybe you're calming them or easing any pain. Maybe just being by their side will be the comfort you both need. Notice you there in that scene being so very peaceful, wrapping your love around them and feeling their love surrounding you, letting them know you're right there with them and together you can do this.
Stroke them, tell them you love them, thank them and let

them know you will always remember them. Give them permission to let go if they need that.

Step 7 - If your beliefs allow then imagine one or more people who have passed away coming forward to welcome your dog into their arms. Listen as they tell you that they'll look after your friend until the time when you can be together again. Give your dog encouragement to go and say that you'll see them again when the time is right.
Watch your dog, with a wagging tail, in the fullest of health again and with your love around them, heading off on this new, wonderful adventure.

Step 8 - Float back into the here and now, take a few more of your calm breaths and when you're ready open your eyes again.

When They Go Suddenly

Albie was eleven but still full of bounce, like a puppy in many ways. One of the things he loved best was playing with his ball and he hadn't realised or just didn't care that the ball was now gently thrown just a few feet away from him and only for a handful of times. It was still the best game ever as he won it every time.

Then one autumn morning as the leaves floated down in the sunlight, with his tail wagging, he caught the ball with triumph and then gently crumpled to the ground. As his human friends rushed to his side there was nothing they could do. His heart had given up as theirs broke.

When a dog dies suddenly, with little or no warning, the shock can be immense.

Although it may have been the best way for them to go it leaves us with no time to prepare or say goodbye. We can't accept or get ready for what's about to happen so we're left reeling in shock and disbelief, our minds desperately trying to unscramble some sense and catch up.

If this is something that you've been through I'm so sorry. For your dog's sake it may well have been a blessing but for yours I can only imagine how hard it must have been.

With something so unexpected and devastating and no time for final words or strokes we need some way to find peacefulness.

When, some weeks later, I met with Albie's family we imagined them going back to the morning of that last day, having a cuddle and a chat with him and asking him what would make his final moments the very best.

It was no surprise to them that they imagined him saying "To be with you and playing with my ball"

He didn't want a sad day, just the best day like all the others with them. He didn't want to have a long illness and lots of trips to the vets. He wanted to go with a bang. He trusted them so much he knew their love for him would mean they'd want to bear the pain and not him.

With their eyes closed they then pictured spending time that morning telling him how much he meant to them and how amazing their life had been with him. They told him he would always live in their hearts and they were now going to have the best ball game ever. To be fair even a rubbish game by their standards was still the best game for him.

For Albie's family they were able to take comfort knowing that he'd been at his happiest in his final moments and I know for many others they may not have had this reassurance and instead an end that wasn't so joyful for their dog.

However that time may have been for you and your friend the shock of their sudden departure may still be an immensely difficult time to process.

Whatever happened that day try this:

When you can take some private moments, by yourself or with someone else who shares or understands your pain, close your eyes and acknowledge how you're feeling. Allow tears to fall if they need to. Out loud or in your head imagine talking to your dog and telling them about the emotions going on inside you.

Tell them what you need them to hear. Maybe it's that

you're sorry you weren't with them or couldn't save them. Maybe you're worried they were in pain or distress. It could be that you're angry with yourself or them, desperately lonely without them, wishing there had been a chance to say goodbye or missing them with all your heart.

Whatever it is keep the thoughts and words flowing and imagine, if they could talk, what they would say to you in all their beautiful wisdom.

Then imagine, if you could change something, how you would have liked their last moments to have been instead.

Maybe you would have been by their side or given them some last moments of joy, like Albie. A ball game or a treat or a cuddle.

See them having that precious time in as much detail as you can imagine. Make it wonderful. Put sounds of happiness in and step into that moment so you're there with them. Thank them for being part of your life and let them know you will love them for always.

Into Their Safekeeping

When we've played a significant part in looking after our dog and they've relied on us for their well-being it can be incredibly difficult to set them free, alone, for their onward journey.

When normally we would have been by their side or given them into the care of someone we trusted, especially if it's somewhere they've never been before, it can be deeply distressing to think of them now by themselves.

I know with our dog, Poppy, I've always explained in detail what her needs are before entrusting her to someone else's care. It's always been so important to know that she'll be happy and loved until we're with her again.

When the times have come to leave her with the carer, for a week or two or even just a day, I've told Poppy I love her, she's a good girl, to stay there and I'll see her in a minute. I've then seen the carer giving her fuss and distracting her while I slip away. While we've been apart her carer has sent loads of photos of our dog looking very happy and relaxed so my mind is put at ease.

Whenever I've gone to pick her up again she's been overjoyed to see me but also extremely happy and settled with the carer. So much so that I think her ideal world would be if my partner and I moved in with her carer too so we could all be together.

If you're feeling distressed that your dog is now, or will be, alone with no-one to look after them may I suggest you try this...

When the time comes to say goodbye to your dog, or even if it happened a while ago and you're still picturing them by themselves or unhappy, think of someone you know who's passed away who you know would so love your friend and be delighted to look after them for you.

If you can't think of anyone who would love and care for them as much as you would don't worry as I've got just the person for you and I'll tell you about him in a minute.

When it's safe to do so close your eyes.

If this heavenly carer had never met your dog in this lifetime imagine telling them everything you'd like them to know about your friend. They'll already know them anyway but it will help to put your own mind at peace.

They'll be taking the most loving care of this precious soul, placed in their safekeeping, until the day comes when they'll be there to hand them back to you.

Get a sense of letting your dog know that this wonderful person will be looking after them for a while and you'll still be loving and missing them everyday but will know that they're being held in love and nurtured so beautifully until you're together again.

Tell them that they're a good boy or girl and to stay there, have loads of fun and you'll see them soon. Then gently hand them over, tenderly with love.

If it would help you then imagine asking the carer to send an image to your mind of your dog every now and then looking so well and healed, and extremely happy. And peaceful in the knowledge that they'll be running back into your arms again one day.

If there isn't anyone you can think of who you'd fully trust to take care of your dog for now then I have someone ready and so very willing, waiting in the wings. And his name is Paul O'Grady.

In case you haven't heard of him he was a very well

known and much loved comedian, broadcaster, drag queen, actor and writer. Many people, including me, got to know and love him even more for his deep love of animals and his campaigning work for their rights.

He became an ambassador for the Battersea Dogs and Cats Home and hosted a tv programme set there called "For The Love Of Dogs". As I write this the new veterinary hospital there is now being named after him.

Animals seemed to quickly sense that he was going to help them and he connected with them with such warmth and love, gentleness and humour that it was beautiful to watch.

He died while I was writing this book and I so wish I'd had the chance to meet him. I am sure that right now he's surrounded by dogs and his heart is so huge that there is always room to welcome and look after another and another and another. And somehow, in wherever Heaven is, time and capacity work differently and Paul will be giving his undivided attention to every single dog who needs him for however long that may be.

If you haven't ever seen his work at Battersea a quick search on the internet should bring up some clips or episodes of "For The Love Of Dogs" and you can see his connection with dogs for yourself.

And, even if you do have a wonderful person ready to welcome your own dog, Paul would be another amazing person to help them settle in. I know that when it's time for us to say goodbye to Poppy I'll be asking Paul to be one of the sets of loving arms she's taken into.

In Their Memory

They bring so much happiness into our lives and when they go they leave behind a dog-shaped hole.

Doing something in their memory and passing on some of that happiness can help fill that hole, even if it's just a little bit.

Remembering Them

~ Gathering other people together to remember and celebrate your dog can be so up-lifting.

When we share the love and the grief we're not so alone and lost and it gives us a space that's safe to share how we're really feeling.

Having a celebration every year to mark their birthday, the day they became your dog or the day they died can bring a tangible time to focus your thoughts. It can be all of those dates if you need or a monthly celebration.

A lovely thing to do is a celebratory walk with others around your dog's favourite routes. Go and play ball where they used to, wade through the streams they splashed through and spend time giving a tour of their very best sniffing and rolling places.

This is somewhere too where social media can be supportive. When we post a photo of our dog on one of their anniversaries people have a chance to offer some words of love and comfort and just for those moments others join us in missing our dog.

. . .

~ Make a book about them - It doesn't have to be to a professional standard although there are many companies who will help you with that if you like. Include as many photos as you can, write down their favourite games, what made them special, their idiosyncrasies and how they changed your life in some way.

~ Put the funniest photo of them that you have somewhere you'll see it every day - if you can find one that makes you laugh or smile then you will still be remembering them but with a happier emotion instead of just pain.

~ Be like them in some way for a day, apart from sniffing bottoms or going to the toilet in public - it could be the way they stretched every time they got up. Or maybe the way they welcomed each new person coming into the room, or forgave quickly. Keep their memory and teachings alive.

Giving In Their Memory

~ Random acts of kindness help not only others but us too. Kindness releases oxytocin, known as the love hormone, and also dopamine, a chemical messenger that gives us a feeling of euphoria. It also increases serotonin, a neurotransmitter that helps regulate mood. All of those things will have been in plentiful supply while your dog was alive but very likely run dry now.

So being kind on behalf of your dog will honour them, give to others and help you as well.

. . .

These are some ideas inspired by those who've felt like you do...

~ Find all of their balls or buy some new ones, put them into a bag and hang it on the gate to a field where dogs love to go. Put up a note, maybe with a photo of your friend beside it, to say your dog would love others to have fun in their memory.

~ Give whichever of their belongings, that you can bear to part with, to a dog in need. Their spare food, toys, bed, towels can continue to be used and enjoyed after they no longer need them. There are many animal charities often in desperate need or maybe someone you know would welcome some things for their dog.

~ Run or walk, in their name, for charity. One thing dogs make us do is go out and walk in the rain or sun, whether we feel like it or not. And when they're gone it can be really hard to find the purpose behind a walk or the motivation to go out on a freezing cold day across muddy fields. But if you found a new reason, to raise money for a charity, by either walking or running it's easier to get back outside.

If you decided to choose a charity that had a connection with helping dogs, and you also did the walks or runs in your dog's memory, then your relationship with your sofa may lose some of its hold on you.

. . .

~ Help out at a dog rescue centre - when you've shared part of your life with a dog you'll understand how some company, stroking and connection can help not only the dog but you too. Every time you go there, every stroke you give, do it on behalf of the friend you lost.

~ Donate the money you would have spent on their food for a month to a dog charity - they will be so grateful and you'll know that a dog is being fed on your loved one's behalf.

Walk Four
Facing Uncomfortable Things

As if the death of a dog isn't hard enough to cope with, along come other challenges.

Guilt is a huge one that so often pushes in to get alongside and then in front of the sadness and is persistent in finding evidence to rest its case.

The reactions of others, often meant in the best way, can push us further down into despair or make us believe we're not normal.

And then there are the things that we don't miss about our dog but can hardly bear to be honest with ourselves about as it feels like a betrayal.

But when we take the hands of these uncomfortable thoughts and feelings, listen to what they're trying to say, and find a way to make peace then we can free ourselves to be in a softer grief.

Shall we turn now and, with compassion, face what I think is one of the hardest emotions, guilt?

Guilt

It's the whisper in your head, the cold hand in your heart. The desperate wish to turn back time, the pleading to have just one more chance to do it differently.

When we can no longer change something, when there are no more days ahead to put things right, and all we have are times to look back on, that's when the door is left wide open for guilt to slide in.

Some of the regrets can come immediately after we've said goodbye to our dogs or can creep in, bit by bit, over time.

We go over in our minds whether we let them go too soon or kept them alive too long. Whether we could have given them more love and attention or noticed sooner that something was wrong.

There's also a heavy weight of guilt if we hadn't been by their side when they died or, even if we have, then somehow not given them a loving and peaceful passing.

Guilt can also accompany any relief we feel if we're thankful that their suffering is over or we're no longer tied as a nurse to their sides. We begin to come down from the state of alert we may have been in with a sick dog or any challenges of looking after them when their personality had changed with illness or age. And with that relief, arm in arm, arrives guilt.

Hindsight is a wonderful thing and so many of us would go back and do things differently if we could. I know for sure, looking back on my life with the wisdom I have now, there are many times that I wish I could change.

But all we had was our knowledge in that moment. And

when we look back it's too easy to forget the reasons why we made the decisions that we did, what was going on in our lives at the time or what we were thinking and feeling back then.

Guilt is a necessary emotion if we really have done something wrong - it helps us to not make the same mistakes again, to apologise, put it right and be accepted back into our tribe or community. But the problem is that many of us take the mistake we made and blow it up out of proportion. We focus on that one time we messed up and don't see the hundreds or thousands of other times when we got it right. And, because it's normally about something in the past that we can't change, it brings with it a feeling of utter helplessness and hopelessness.

We play the things we did wrong over and over in our minds, making the images life-size, with sound, movement and colour. We'll add in the "If Onlys" and then torture ourselves that we didn't take that path instead. Looking back it was a sliding door moment and we took the wrong one.

Something that is remarkable about dogs is that they live so much more in the moment than we do. If a dog has stolen some human food or ripped up a cushion he or she may look guilty when we discover the offence an hour later but I think that's because they're reacting to our voice and expression in the present time. They know we're cross but don't put two and two together. They don't seem to understand the consequences of their actions after the event and so I believe that frees them from the guilt that we go through.

Earlier today I was walking with my dog Poppy in the woods. We've never managed to train her not to eat things that she finds on the ground, like a stranger's tissue or a discarded food wrapper. And today was no exception. She grabbed something lying amongst the fallen leaves and as I shouted for her to drop it she reverted to a playful puppy having the most amazing game. The more I told her to drop it the more she danced and pranced and ran around, just out of my reach. If dogs could laugh she would have been in absolute hysterics.

Meanwhile all I could do was imagine it was something dangerous and see us having to rush to the vets.

Some years ago I knew a gorgeous dog called Bailey who had a huge appetite for swallowing gloves, unopened packets of tissues or anything highly dangerous for a dog to eat and he had so many trips to the vets he should have had a season ticket. Did he ever feel any guilt? I think that's highly unlikely.

So with Poppy dancing around today and eventually either dropping or swallowing whatever it was I felt pretty cross that she hadn't done as I'd asked. And just like when you're in a huff with a person I marched out of the woods, ignoring her plaintive stare to now play in the stream with her.

As I strode purposefully along she realised she was in trouble and fell into step right behind me. And with each step I realised she had no idea what she'd done wrong. The prancing, dancing, eating something she shouldn't have incident was long forgotten in her mind. She had no guilt whatsoever about it so there was no point, and it suddenly just felt mean, staying in a strop.

Guilt can be so overwhelming it smothers the wonderful memories of the times we shared with our dog and that's such a shame.

Our dogs want us to be happy and if we allow them to be our teachers, even after they're gone, they can lead us to a more comfortable way of being, journeying between the present and a more balanced view of the past.

What to do

Here are some ideas to help find peace with the guilt.

Welcome in the guilt

Very often the feelings that we have that are less than good become even stronger when we try to ignore them or fight them or allow them to push us around.

Take a moment now to be with how you're feeling. Imagine opening the door to that emotion and, instead of trying to argue with it or shutting the door in its face or letting it push you down, quietly and calmly allow it in and invite it to take a seat. Let that feeling know that you will listen to what it's trying to say and that you will be able to hear it best when it talks kindly and doesn't shout in an accusing way.

Take as long as you need. It may be a few seconds or several minutes but listen as objectively as you can.

Thank the guilt for whatever it's been trying to tell you. Let it know you've heard it.

If it had a good intention behind it what would it be trying to do? Maybe it's making sure you don't do something similar again that you'll regret or it feels you need to put something right?

Is there a way to learn from the mistakes you think you made and for which you feel so guilty?

If a similar situation arose in the future would you do something differently?

Is there something you need to do to make amends or show you're sorry in any way? Maybe an act of kindness for another dog so that some good comes from this?

Is this a chance, however painful it's been, that your wisdom has now deepened because of what you think you did wrong? Is it possible you are now a better person in some way than you were before?

Once you've listened to the guilt, and it has nothing left to say, thank it and politely show it out of the door again.

If it needs to come back at any time then repeat what you've done, listening, learning, thanking it and showing it out again. Over time its visits will likely become less frequent until the day comes when it shows up at your door and you can just open it, nod in recognition and watch it turn away again.

Welcome yourself to court

When we're giving ourselves a hard time, particularly with guilt, it's so normal to swing the bias against ourselves. We become our own Prosecution lawyers, doing our utmost to prove ourselves guilty of the crime, providing plenty of evidence for a weighty conviction. Most of the time we never think to bring in Defence lawyers or if we do it's someone just out of college with such a faint voice they can hardly be heard.

So, unless you've done something deliberately and know-ingly cruel to your dog, how about we make it a more balanced case?

If it helps then bring in someone whose opinion you trust or, if it feels more comfortable, you can do this by yourself.

If you have someone else with you ask them to take the

part of the Defence because, most likely, you'll be an expert as the Prosecution.

Or, if you're doing this alone, you can take both roles but each must be as dedicated and strong as the other. You may need to put more effort into the part of the Defence because the opposite probably comes more naturally.

First of all make your case, as the Prosecution, to show why you're guilty. State all the facts against you that you can think of and then rest your case.

Next, either you or someone else, as your Defence make the case to show your innocence. Bring in any mitigating circumstances, previous good behaviour, and as many examples as possible to show when you did the opposite of the guilty behaviour in the past. Then rest your case.

As your own Judge and Jury how do you now find yourself? Still guilty as previously charged or understood and forgiven? Maybe even with nothing to forgive apart from being human and messing up as we all do.

Welcome your dog

Imagine calling your dog to your side as you tell them what you feel so bad about and wish had been different.

If it feels too painful then talk about yourself in the third person. Instead of "I" use "she" or "he".

So "She so wishes that she hadn't gone out shopping that day and been there when you died. If she could turn back time she'd have asked her neighbour to pick up some food instead so she could have stayed behind with you."

Float into the mind of your dog and see through their eyes this very moment in time when they're with you and you're the best thing ever. See all of the times when you were there with them. The middle of the night excursions when they were a puppy and toilet training, the walks slipping through the mud when you didn't feel like it, the games when you'd rather be reading a book, the reassuring cuddles as fireworks lit the sky, the gentle strokes when you knew they were feeling unwell.

From their heart feel the unconditional love flowing back and forth to yours and hear their thoughts that one small moment in all those times doesn't matter. It was the whole life together that counted, not the final hours. They knew and still know that they are loved.

Now, in honour of your dog and to be in your own present moment, is it time yet to thank the guilt and gently let it go?

When Others Don't Understand

*"It's six weeks now since Honey died and I'm still crying. I
think some people think I'm being slightly daft but I loved her
so much. I'm afraid now to mention the pain I'm in. My
friends are either changing the subject when I talk about her
or reminding me she was a dog and not a person."*

Even if other people don't say the words it may well be that
you can see them thinking "It was just a dog".

If only that were true. If it was just a dog you could go
out the same day, find another one, forget this one and save
yourself a world of sadness. But then you would have missed
out on all the love and the relationship that has led to this
pain.

Others react in all sorts of ways when grief is around and
it's worth understanding and being prepared for the different
reactions you may encounter.

In a similar way to when a person dies many people are
often left floundering for the right things to say. They may
have good intentions and try and minimise your loss so you
don't feel so bad. "It was just a dog" is their way of saying
"Cheer up, it doesn't matter that much, so you don't need to
hurt so much"

They might not say anything as they don't want to upset
you and believe it's a subject best left alone.

Or they may try and change the subject to take your
mind off your sadness.

The intentions here are usually kind and for some people
they're just what's needed in that moment. In fact, personally, if I'm only just holding it together then anyone offering

sympathy will tip me over the edge and that might not be at an appropriate time.

It may come as a surprise but some people may even start arguing with you when you try to explain the relationships people can have with their dogs. They will lecture you that dogs aren't humans and how can you possibly compare it or even say the grief is worse losing your dog than it was with a member of your family? This is especially true if someone is grieving over a friend or family member who has recently died. They may well feel shocked and even angry that you could liken your own pain to theirs.

But all you probably needed was someone to say how genuinely sorry they were and, even if they'd never had a dog, to tell you that they can see it must have been a very special relationship.

Other well-meaning people may keep checking up on how you're doing because they genuinely care and want you to know they're thinking of you. If you're only just gasping for air amongst the grief it may feel easier to not even reply as you're desperately trying not to think about it and answering their concerns will pull you back down. Unless that person understands this they may become even more worried about you if you don't reply or even feel rejected.

What to do

Be very sensitive about sharing the depth of your feelings with anyone who has recently lost a human loved one, even more so if they have never loved and lost a dog. It may well cause the foundations of your relationship to crumble. Try not to compare your own loss with theirs. No-one's grief is exactly the same anyway, whether it's for a person or a dog so do your utmost to open your heart to whatever they're going through and find for yourself someone who isn't in their own grief and who understands the pain that comes from losing a dog and can comfort you in your sadness.

Remember that whatever someone says or any avoidance of your grief may well come from kindness and their belief in what's right.

It will also come from their own experience, whether or not they've ever loved a dog, and also from their upbringing and the way they handle sadness and loss. Maybe they were brought up to hide their tears or have the belief that dogs are just animals?

Tell someone what it is you need right now. If they are trying to offer advice or 'fix" the problem and it's not helping then gently tell them you really appreciate what they're trying to do and it would be far more helpful if they just listened while you told them about your dog.

If you need to be able to hold things together for a while and any mention of your dog will set you off then ask them to talk about other things for now and you'll let them know when it's safe for you to open that door again.

If someone really doesn't understand what you're feeling then try not to take it personally. It's unlikely they're being cruel. Maybe loving an animal and having that deep connection is like a foreign language to them and they just can't speak or understand it. There may come a day when they'll find themselves in the same position and you'll be able to offer comfort and understanding to them instead.

For now, thank them for their words and move away or change the conversation.

Seek out those who have been through something similar or at least currently have a dog who they love. They will have an understanding of the same language and may even be fluent in it.

There are many online communities for people grieving pets who are ready to support you. A quick search online will bring some up. Have a look and see if there is one that feels right for you. Sometimes talking to strangers in similar situations can be comforting and you'll know these other people truly understand.

In the UK the Blue Cross offers Pet Bereavement and Pet Loss support as do many other charities and it's really worth getting in touch if you need to talk to someone. Many other Countries have similar helpful societies and groups. There are often online communities or phone support so you could access them from anywhere in the world.

Above all hold onto the knowledge that the bond you shared with your dog was real, the love was and is deep, the pain is normal. It's lovely and comforting when others know the best things to say to you but, even if they don't, it doesn't diminish what you had. Maybe one day they too will go on the emotional journey that you have and then they will understand.

The Things We Don't Miss

When someone we love dies we tend to focus mostly on the good things about them. It feels wrong to talk or even think badly of the dead and while that's kind, as they can no longer defend themselves, it can leave the memory of the relationship we had with them as not fully real.

It can be the same with our dogs too when they go. We can easily turn them into saints and forget the times when they annoyed us or the things that, hand on heart, we actually don't miss.

And just like with the people we've lost, remembering everything about our dogs, the good and the not so good, is ok. It doesn't mean we don't miss them with all our hearts or desperately want them back, even if they still do the annoying thing. It just proves that we loved them, the whole of them, despite these things.

It's easy to love another being if they're flawless but humans and dogs are rarely perfect and the fact that we still adore them even though there were things we wanted to change shows the depths that our love grew.

If it helps make you feel more normal here are some of the things that other people don't miss about their dogs. Every single one of them though weeps that their dog is no longer here and would happily have them back, even with their faults.

~ Barking at delivery drivers
~ Terrifying the Postie
~ Waking you up in the middle of the night to go out
~ The extra cost of food, vets, dog care
~ Not being able to be spontaneous

~ Mud in the house
~ Dog hair in the house
~ Walking when we don't feel like it
~ The worry when they're ill
~ The house being destroyed by teething or weeing, pooing puppies
~ Always putting our dogs first
~ Hogging the bed
~ Chasing cats
~ Pulling on the lead
~ Stealing food
~ Eating poo
~ Rolling in poo
~ Being lead aggressive
~ Attention seeking

If you find yourself not missing something about your dog even though you loved them then rejoice that this shows just how much they really meant to you.

Other Relationships

I just don't feel the same about my wife anymore since our dog died. I needed to take my time, keep some of his things and, the day he died, she took them all down to the dump without asking me. I am so lonely in my marriage and my dog was my comforter in all times.

Now I look at him over the supper table and I can't bear the thought that it was actually our dog holding us together all this time. I can't even think of anything to say to him anymore.

In an ideal world you and the significant people in your life would have been in harmony preparing for your dog's passing and supporting each other in the days afterwards. But times like these can bring the shock that sometimes relationships are not ideal and that we think and deal very differently to others in how we cope.

The impact of your dog dying can reach far into relationships. A dog may have been the glue that held you and your partner together, very much like children, something in common, to talk and care about, to share.

Or they may have covered up for something lacking, been that listening ear, the one who made you feel worthwhile, the bringer of love and smiles.

Even after your dog has gone one of you may want to

hold onto their belongings while the other needs to let go of them straight away.

You may want to talk continuously about them while your partner finds it too painful to mention them at all.

Resentment can burst out if you didn't agree on the treatment your dog received or whether it was the right time to let them go.

The cracks in relationships that had been filled so beautifully by your furry friend now stare you straight in the face, just at a time when you don't have the emotional strength to know what to do.

Friendships too can suffer when those you thought would understand and be supportive show a lack of empathy. The comfort you desperately crave and believed would be there is nowhere to be found and you can see friends in a different, unkinder light which shines straight onto values that don't align with yours.

Very often there's a lot of anger after we lose a dog and that can so easily be directed at someone close to us.

When we're in pain we're raw, vulnerable, highly sensitive and often unable to think and act rationally. Our emotional brain hijacks our rational part and we can over-react if others break the rapport or don't show compassion to us.

We can also be so inside ourselves surviving in our grief that we have no spare capacity to give to others who then no longer see us as the best version of ourselves.

Within a family each person will have had their own, slightly different, relationship with your dog and be showing their emotions, burying them deep inside, feeling it deeply or maybe not much at all.

Add in some blame and guilt hurtling around and the ground can begin shifting dangerously.

So, what can be done?

If we were in an ideal world everyone would say how they're feeling whilst being really listened to and understandings would be reached with huge compassion. The terrible loss of your dog could be the beginning of deeper, more loving connections.

But here in the real world there are often already difficulties and miscommunications within relationships and with sensitivities running high it can be a challenge to know what to do.

When your dog has recently passed grief can be so overwhelming and take people by surprise. We cope in our own ways and these could be in stark contrast to how someone else seems to be doing.

While this isn't a book about human relationships there are a few things that may be worth trying...

Before you start there are some gentle guidelines to keep in mind that will help.

Some important words to be careful using when you're talking to someone, unless you're being complimentary, are "always" and "never". If they're used in a critical way they can come across as attacking the whole person and provoke a defensive attack back.

Be specific about a situation rather than generalising. So rather than "You never seem to care when I'm upset' say "When I started crying yesterday you walked away. Why did you need to do that?"

Try not to time travel. Wherever possible talk about

recent times not something that happened long ago. The other person may not remember it, history can distort our perceptions and when it's long in the past it's very difficult to do anything to make it right.

Take responsibility for how you're feeling rather than pointing a finger of blame at someone else. Instead of saying "You make me feel..." try "When you say that I then feel...".

Hard as it may be try and step inside the other person to see if you can understand what they're thinking.

If it's possible ask them to explain how they're feeling. Listen, without jumping in, and repeat back to them a summary of what they've said, so they know you've really heard them.

If they don't then ask you how you're feeling see, without attacking or criticising them, if they're open to you explaining it. In a loving relationship you'd both listen and really hear how the other is doing and find some ways forward that are best for you both. When there are challenges or sensitivities sometimes the best way forward is to respect each other's position in ways that are as kind as possible and find compromises where you can.

Imagine that one person doesn't want to think or talk about the dog that's gone whilst the other desperately needs to keep their memory alive. It seems like an impossible situation that neither will budge from and it's causing even more pain in a situation full of sadness.

Or maybe one person is on a search for another dog to fill the hole while the other can't bear the thought of it.

If the situation feels too difficult to even begin listening and talking in this way maybe there's a neutral third party who can help, a friend or relative who can keep things calm and encourage you to hear the other person?

By talking and really listening to each other to find out why each one feels the way they do there's hope that, even if you both still feel the same as you did before, you can have some understanding of where the other is right now and feel heard and understood.

So if you want to keep your dog's memory alive and your partner can't bring themselves to talk about them or see any reminders maybe a way forward would be to try and respect that this may be just the way they feel right now and understand their pain. You could make a memory box that you keep out of their sight, look at photos when they're not there and find someone else to talk to about your dog.

While this isn't ideal it may just be a temporary situation and in a few months your partner may begin mentioning them again once the rawness has faded.

Or if one person in your family is on an urgent hunt for another dog let them know you understand and see if they would be alright to give it a few months and then you promise you'll think about it properly once you can think straight again.

With your significant other, if your dog was the bond holding you together, and loneliness is there now instead, when the time feels right, try bringing up memories from the time when you first met and fell in love with your partner. We can lose each other along the way and, because a dog can be such an amiable companion, it's often easier to direct our love to them. But at the beginning, hopefully, you felt a connection with your partner. When you begin to remember who you both were when you met and what drew you together there's a chance that you can now re-kindle some of that. There's an empty space now begging to be filled with love.

Talk about how you felt when you first got together, the good things that you saw in them, all that you still admire and love. We can get into the habit of taking those closest to us for granted or just seeing their faults and what we focus on we get more of.

I wonder what would happen if you both took a moment, now there isn't a wet nose trying to nudge for attention, and looked at each other with compassion? To really see the person from the days when you first met, who is maybe still there waiting to be discovered again.

With friendships, particularly with those who've never loved and lost a dog, imagine that it's like a foreign language that they've never learnt and they genuinely don't understand the pain you're feeling.

You could choose to not share your feelings about your dog with them if they don't seem to understand and use your times together as a brief respite to think and talk about other things.

Or you could see if they're open to hearing how you are and finding a way to support you. This may be a chance for them to grow in wisdom and understanding and for your friendship to deepen.

If you see your relationship in a different, unresolvable way now and it feels like the only answer is to let it go, then thank your friend to their face or in your heart for all that you've shared. Some people come into our lives just for a part of our journey. And sometimes, even many years later, we reconnect again if it's meant to be. It's much easier to open up to each other again if the parting had been kind and loving. And maybe time will have helped them to understand what you were going through.

Walk Five
Other Griefs

The heartache that comes when your dog is no longer here doesn't just come with the aftermath of them dying.

There can be immense grief when a dog goes missing or needs to be re-homed.

Even hearing about a dog you never knew meeting with tragedy can be very hard to cope with.

Each of these deserves a book in their own right but let's have a gentle look at them now...

When Your Dog Goes Missing

As I sit here writing, last night was New Year's Eve and I never imagined I'd spend much of that night joining a search party for a missing dog.

As the church clock struck midnight in our village the people in several of the houses around the church decided to set off their fireworks all at the same time. It was a spectacular display but hugely distressing for a lot of the animals around here. So much so that Maisie, the dog of some nearby neighbours who'd brought her to watch the display, was so terrified that she slipped her lead and bolted away, last seen running past her house and out along the main road with fields on either side.

So until 3.30am the lanes, back gardens and muddy fields had their velvet darkness pierced by people's torches and everywhere we walked we heard the sound of whistling or someone calling out her name.

Some took to their bicycles to cover more ground but she was nowhere to be found. It was with reluctance that the search was called off until daylight and her owners left their front door open just in case.

I watched the darkness from our bedroom window for a while, hoping to see her suddenly reappear by the church but nothing stirred and so, with an uneasy heart, I too went to bed to fitfully sleep.

Her story had a happy ending, thank goodness, as news arrived that just before 7am Maisie had found her own way home, in through the open door, and although very muddy and tired, was unharmed.

Every time I see a post about a missing dog my heart goes out to all those who love them and are desperately searching or waiting and hoping. I often think this must be like living in a suspended grief.

At the time of writing the price of puppies has gone up extortionately here in the UK and there has been a huge increase in dog thefts. But many dogs go missing too without having been stolen.

While this part is about living without knowing where your dog is I'm sharing some ideas if your dog has disappeared recently or a while ago, just in case there's something you hadn't thought of.

What to do if your dog has recently disappeared:

~ Act as fast as you can as you need as much time on your side as possible.

~ If you think your dog may have been stolen then call the police immediately.

~ Call the microchip database your dog is registered with and make sure your contact details are up to date. Tell them that your dog is missing in case anyone else tries to change their details.

~ Ring around local vets, dog wardens, dog charities and rehoming centres and don't worry about being a nuisance. A quick call every so often will keep your dog fresh in their minds.

~ Register your dog on Doglost, a free site reuniting lost, stray and stolen dogs with their owners.

- Battersea Dogs and Cats Home also have a Lost Dogs & Cats Line. Call them on 020 7627 9245. Their website also has some useful information on what to do and a Missing Poster that you can download.

~ Go to the last place you know where they were and leave an item of your unwashed clothing there and keep going back to check if there's been any sign of them.

~ Use social media - if your dog has been stolen then make them too hot to handle. If your dog has just vanished then asking people to share photos and information increases the odds of finding them.

~ Keep on, don't give up. Keep putting the posters up, photos of them with their coat long and short, when they were thinner and plumper, with different expressions. It may be that if someone else has them they've let their coat grow long or had it trimmed short.

~ If it feels right to you then think about offering a reward for information leading to their safe return.

~ Keep searching. Go with others, try and find quiet times and call their name and listen. Take their favourite noisy toy and some treats. Keep leaving items of your clothing in places they might head to and check back regularly.

~ If, after your dog has vanished, you move home then update their microchip details immediately, tell the new residents of the home you're leaving about your missing dog, give them photos and contact numbers for you, just in case.

~ Buy or borrow a drone with a camera. You may need to ask permission to fly it, depending on the area where you live, but it can be a really useful way to cover ground and look for signs. There are also organisations who will use their drones to help look for your dog.

When Time Has Passed

As the days and weeks slip by and there still haven't been any signs of your dog there can be such a collision of emotions taking place. Hope, despair, grief, anger, desperation. The not knowing what has happened is so hard to deal with.

Our minds try to make sense of what's going on and find some way of feeling in control and that's so difficult to do when we don't have all the answers.

If you find you're dreaming more than usual or having strange dreams that's really normal. Your mind is borrowing metaphors that somehow fit the emotions that you're feeling, trying to process and make sense of what's going on in your waking time.

In the few hours of sleep I had when we didn't know where Maisie was I had a dream that I was walking along a motorway, trying to cross it and only just dodging the cars. Even though we don't live near a motorway my mind used this analogy to put me in the danger I believed that Maisie was in and work out how to get across the fast moving traffic and survive.

When more than a few hours have passed since your dog went missing be aware that you're living under ongoing stress and it's highly likely that you're in a prolonged state of fight or flight. Hormones are triggered that prepare us to either stay in a situation and fight or to escape to save our lives. We're only meant to be in this state just for short periods of time.

When we're faced with a physical or psychological danger, whether real or imagined, our body's sympathetic nervous system is activated by the sudden release of hormones. These trigger the adrenal glands to release adrenaline and noradrenaline which then increase our heart rates, blood pressure and rate of breathing. All really vital for a sudden burst of energy we may need. We may also find our legs are trembling as the muscles tense ready for action, like revving a car with the handbrake on. Our digestion can also slow down or temporarily stop so our bodies can divert the energy where it's needed. And we may well feel or be sick or urgently need the toilet. These last two distressing physical reactions are apparently the body's way of being lighter to run away and less tasty to prey.

All this is fine and needed for immediate danger but when we're in a prolonged state of stress, when our dog has been missing for more than just a few minutes, we stay in a state of fight or flight and these physical reactions begin to take their toll. The more you can do to look after yourself at this time the better you will cope.

And if we're not in fight or flight we may well be in a 'freeze' state instead, like rabbits caught in headlights. This can happen before, during, after or instead of fight or flight.

It can also be, under the huge emotional overload when a dog goes missing, that our rational, intelligent brains are hijacked by our emotional brains. Just like when you're put under pressure to remember someone's name and your mind goes blank, but to a much greater extent. With the urgency to work out how to find your dog your mind can feel like it literally can't grasp or understand anything, let alone make any decisions.

Things That May Help

Whether you're in the initial state of fight, flight or freeze or it's been going on for a while there are some things that you can do that will help ease the anxiety.

Breathe

When we're calm we can think more clearly and rationally. It may be that an idea you hadn't thought of before pops into your head or you can plan what steps to take next.

Calm breathing is very helpful for slowing down our thoughts and lowering our body's stress response. You'll be sending signals to your brain that it's safe to calm down.

Start with a big sigh out and imagine letting the worry and anxiety out with it.

Take a normal breath in and then allow a few more breaths to follow where the out-breath is longer than the in-breath. Try breathing out for the count of 11 seconds and in for 7. Adjust this to suit your own lungs, making sure the out-breath is longer than the in-breath.

Believe

Keep hope flickering - I've heard of dogs who've been missing for years who are suddenly reunited with their owners. Just today, while writing, I read about a Jack Russell called Lucky who'd been snatched from her owners when they were out walking. Sixteen months later she was found wandering the streets, picked up by a dog warden and taken to Battersea Dogs and Cats Home in London. The staff there checked her microchip, discovered she'd been stolen and reunited her with her owners.

Keep going

Don't give up. Keep on sharing their photos on social media, putting up posters, ringing around vets and animal charities. Keep checking on DogLost and keep going back to where your dog was last seen.

Imagine

Many of us imagine the worst case scenarios when we don't actually know what's happened. Our imaginations are so vivid that we then react physically and emotionally as if it's really happening. Many years ago my partner bought a longed-for motorbike and the next day I waved him off on it on his two hour journey into London. As soon as he was out of sight I started playing horrific scenes in my mind, imagining the police turning up at the door, planning his funeral, the days and years ahead. And I spent the whole day in a terrible state, sobbing my heart out until, as the evening drew in, I heard the sound of his motorbike coming up the road and, as I quickly dried my eyes so he wouldn't know, I saw through the window his beaming face inside his motorbike helmet, back home safe and sound.

I'd lived through a whole day of grieving for no reason at all. I didn't tell him until some years later what had happened that day as I didn't want to spoil his enjoyment of being back on a bike again.

If your dog has gone missing it's the easiest thing in the world to imagine some dreadful fate has befallen them or they're now in uncaring hands. And imagining this will be torture day after day. So, unless thinking this way has a good intention, stirring you into action or motivating you to never give up searching, there may be a kinder way to treat yourself.

Look at what you know for sure. Was your dog stolen? Or did they run away or get lost? Is it possible that they were found or sold on and are now being looked after kindly? Trust me that I know this would still be far from the ideal situation as you just want them safely back home again but if there are no benefits from imagining a worse scenario then the only thing this is doing is keeping you in a waking nightmare.

If you imagine for a moment that, whatever the reason your dog went missing, they are now with someone loving and caring and that one day, somehow, you will be reunited again this may bring you a gentle moment of peace.

Tap

Something else that's really worth having a look at is Emotional Freedom Technique or EFT. It's an emotional version of acupuncture, without the use of needles, and has successfully been used for many physical ailments and, importantly for anyone living under stress, for emotional ones too. If you're interested in finding out more about this there are lots of videos on Youtube with the founder of EFT, Gary Craig, demonstrating how to do it. You can also visit the official EFT website Www.EmoFree.com for a free EFT tutorial.

Love

Send your dog love. Tell them in your mind or out loud that you're not giving up and you're right here loving them still. Imagine your dog feeling that love coming their way and sending their unquestioning love back to you.

Remember

As time goes on and there's still no sign of them, create a time and place for a daily, weekly or monthly "Remembering" by yourself or with others who are part of your dog's greater pack. Talk about ideas or plans to keep searching, gather together to share prayers, wishes or thanks, light a candle of hope, share tears and comfort. Do whatever you need to keep your faith and love as strong as you can and remember that the love between you still connects you and always will.

Grieving When You Give A Dog Away

Grief can come, not only when your dog dies, but if for some reason you have to let them go to another home.

Circumstances change, money can become too tight to look after a dog, sometimes the family dynamic alters or a dog can show signs of aggression.

I often wonder what the story is that's led to a dog being in an animal shelter. There are many reasons and it's not my place to judge. In an ideal world a dog would find a loving home and stay there forever but sadly life's not always like that and heartbreaking choices have to be made.

When you've loved a dog and you have no other option than to re-home them it can be incredibly painful.

If you're facing this decision right now then may I offer some words of experience in a moment?

If it's something that happened in the past then I'd love to show you some ways to heal the pain.

I'm going to share my own story first and give you a window in so you can see how I make it a little less painful for myself.

Oliver

When I was two or three years old a golden retriever arrived in our lives, called Oliver. Looking back I'm guessing he was a few months old as he wasn't a tiny puppy. He was very friendly, didn't understand he mustn't bound up to little children in the playground, loved our cats, was completely untrained, went everywhere with us and quickly became one of the family. And we adored him.

I was eight when my parents split up and a year or so later my mum met a new man who became our stepfather. And so, along with our cats, Oliver had to be re-homed.

As children we had no say in keeping him and my sister and I joined our mum on the final walk with Oliver, before taking him with her to the animal charity and saying goodbye. As I remember his face now, innocently watching us go, my heart feels so painful.

When we got back home we weren't allowed to shed tears or show that we missed him or were sad and had to carry on as if nothing had happened. We never knew who had re-homed him.

If my mum were alive now I'd talk to her about it, ask her if she tried to find a home for him with someone we knew. Or if she considered re-homing our step-father instead which many of us think would have been a far better option.

But life often works out differently than we'd thought and sometimes there are unanswered questions and unresolved pain.

And so I'm taking a pause now to bring him back to mind. Beautiful Oliver. So mad, so exuberant, so lovely.

We took him to a training class once when we first got him but I think my mum was so embarrassed by his frolics that we never went back. Remembering our walks, how he was always there, wherever we were, how he and our adopted stray cat Tabitha had a wonderful bond, sleeping together, going on walks together and Oliver letting her kittens ride on his back.

And I'm saying thank you to him for showing me from an early age how dogs can be such an important part of the tapestry of the family.

Now I need to say sorry. So, so sorry Oliver that we couldn't keep you. As hot tears fall from my eyes I weep for him and weep that we were helpless as children to speak up.

Angry that my sister and I didn't run away with him or ask our mum to really think what she was being made to do. Or turn to our relatives and friends and say "Can't you have him please?"

And now the adult me gently steps in and reminds me that there was nowhere else for him to go. And if we'd begged to keep him then his life with us, with a step-father who didn't want him, would never have been like it had been before. That there were days before that decision to re-home him, when he was left in our old house alone and visited just for quick walks and food. His life had already changed and knowing the years that lay ahead for us all there was no way it would have been a good life for him.

So I close my eyes now and imagine. I bring to life a scene of what might have happened after we said goodbye to him at the re-homing centre.

In my mind, as we drive away another car drives in. Inside are a really friendly looking couple and their teenage children who've recently lost their dog. They are so heartbroken and lost and in desperate need of a dog to fill that hole.

As they make their way to reception they pass by Oliver in his pen and stop to say hello. And as they do he runs over to the wire to greet them, tail wagging, and they look at each other and know they've found their dog.

I float unseen into later on that day as they arrive with him at their home, his new home, and they show him around. They have toys ready for him, a bowl of water and one filled with his favourite food and a really comfy looking bed. But they'll let him come upstairs with them just for that night and sleep on their beds, to settle in. As it will turn out it will actually be every night after that he'll be allowed to sleep up there too, just in case he feels lonely. They already adore him and his beautiful face lights up as knows now this is where he belongs.

I'll say goodbye for now Oliver. I'll miss you and love you always. Thank you for being part of my childhood.

If I feel that pain of sadness at any time I will imagine him in this life with his new family, running through the fields and woods with them, with his boundless energy, being with them wherever they go. Belonging and loved.

If you're facing this decision right now and need to find a new home for your dog please take a moment and some care to make the right and kindest choice. Your dog is completely dependant on you.

Take a few calm breaths and work out if this needs to be a temporary or permanent solution. Calmness allows us to think more clearly and a situation that may have felt hopeless may actually have a solution somewhere.

Maybe It's a Temporary Solution You Need

Have you suddenly become really busy or need to be away from home more than usual?

Do you need help with dog walking or over-night care and just can't afford it? If so have a look at a site called Borrow My Doggy. For a small annual fee your dog can be matched with someone who loves dogs but isn't in a position to have their own. Even though there are vetting procedures to go through I have always done my own checks too, going for several dog walks with a new borrower and then taken my dog to their house so I know where they live. Only when I feel confident that they understand what Poppy needs and how to look after her would I consider letting her go off alone with them. She and we have made some life-long relationships through this site. In fact a few years ago Poppy was a flower girl at one couple's wedding who had come into her life as "Borrowers" and turned into wonderful friends.

Ask around neighbours, friends, relatives to see if anyone can help. You may be surprised who would be happy to have your dog with them for some of the day or over-night or who just needs an excuse for a walk.

If money is the problem then the pdsa, Blue Cross and RSPCA may be able to offer help with veterinary costs. The Dogs Trust runs some wonderful schemes too - Hope Project, which helps the dogs of homeless people and also Freedom Project, which offers foster care for those fleeing domestic violence. Give them a call and see what help they can give.

Over the last few years food banks have sprung up to help people feed their pets. It's really worth checking in your area to see if there's help in this way. I would be tempted too, if I really couldn't feed my dog, to swallow my pride and ask everyone I knew if they could spare some food or a donation to buy some. Recently one of our neighbours asked if anyone had any old blankets for a local dog charity she helped at and the response was immense. I found myself not only digging out old sheets and blankets but also going and buying bags and boxes of food. She posted a photo a few days after her appeal showing heaps of blankets, toys, treats and loads of food. People like to help and there are a lot of dog lovers out there who would do all that they could to help your dog stay with you if possible.

Another idea is a dog share. This may sound strange but

if you and another family, who both love your dog, split looking after her and all of the costs it may be that you won't have to say goodbye completely. I know for sure that our Poppy would very happily live for a few days every week with some of her special friends and then be delighted to be home with us again. Every dog is different but it's worth considering if your dog is sociable and forms a close bond with others. They will still love you just as much, honestly.

If It's a Permanent Solution You Need

Life changes rapidly and sometimes, however much we wish it were different, there's no choice but to find a new home for your dog.

I would urge the utmost caution if you're considering putting your dog up for free or even for sale on a public site. Whilst most people have good hearts there are some that don't.

If you already happen to know someone who has been longing for a dog and you know they would give them a good home then that could be a wonderful solution. You'd need to work out if you'll have any contact with your dog after they've been re-homed. Please, unless you're going to share them, see them regularly or have them back again, however much you may want to still see them, if you believe it would unsettle them then put their wellbeing first. It may be that once they've been with their new family long enough they can see you again but in a new way as wonderful, familiar visitors.

If you do decide to go down this route then, if it's possible, let their new owners come and meet them a few times and go for walks with you. Go to their home with your dog several times too so they get used to it. Then at least when it's time for your final goodbye your dog will have people and a place that they're familiar with.

Take an item of clothing with the new owners' smells on it from their home and give it to your dog before you meet which will help with the bonding. And when it's time to take them and hand them over then leave them with something that has your scent on it to make them feel at home.

Sometimes the best solution can be found at an animal charity. There are some well respected ones such as the Blue Cross and Dogs Trust who are just a phone call away. They shouldn't judge, will talk you through what happens and will be very mindful about who your dog gets re-homed with. I can never understand why any animal gets abandoned when these places are there.

Whichever path you choose here are some thoughts to make it as loving and as peaceful as possible to say goodbye...

Have a best day ever for your dog. If you can then take them somewhere you know that they love, give them all your attention and love and take photos. In the moments before you pass them over to their new home give them loads of praise and thank them for being a wonderful part of your life and that you'll always remember them. Wish them well and imagine your love being wrapped around them as you hand them over.

Once you've left them allow whatever feelings are there to come out. You may feel numb or relieved and that's ok. You may want to bawl your eyes out, so do. Keep reminding yourself why you needed to do this and keep sending love and wishing your dog well.

Helping Children Let Their Dog Go

Depending on the age of your children, their personalities and relationship to your dog there are some things which will make the parting easier and the future more bearable for them.

If you believe that there is no chance of holding onto your dog then, as soon as you can and while your dog is still living with you, explain to your children why they need to go. Allow them to question you, listen to them, answer them as best you can and let them express their emotions.

Thinking back to when we had to let Oliver go it would have helped immensely if our mum had talked things through with us beforehand. We could have suggested people we knew who may take him on, asked her to really think whether our step-father was worth giving up our dog for, and at the very least been in on the thought processes right from the beginning and not when it was too late.

Children, although often naive and idealistic, can sometimes come up with ideas that you hadn't thought of before. But even if not then they will have a chance to understand why you're making this decision and begin their own way of letting go.

Give them as much information as you can about what will happen. If you're taking your dog to a re-homing centre they will normally let you keep in touch while they still have your dog and let you know when a new family has been found. Tell your children how your dog is getting on. Encourage them to draw some pictures or write a list of what your dog likes that you can hand over when you say goodbye so they know the new owners will have a good understanding of their friend.

If you feel sad once your dog has gone don't try and hide it from them. Children need to know it's safe to show emotion and that they can do it too. Take some time together to talk about how you miss them and share wishes about the new family you think they'll end up with. However sad you feel give your children hope and the belief that their dog is happy.

Every night before bed, for as many nights as needed, send love and thoughts or prayers to your dog and let your children know that you're sure their friend is hearing them.

If It Was In The Past

If you're grieving for a dog that you've already had to re-home it's possible that you still need to find some peace with this.

Maybe you know a bit about the new home your dog went to but if you don't then that can leave questions unanswered and worries that eat away.

While an animal rescue centre can't always give you details of your dog's new home they may well, if you get in touch, be able to reassure you.

If you can't find out any information then try what I did with my feelings about Oliver. Close your eyes and imagine the kind of people who you hope are the new owners and the wonderful life your dog is now leading. Remind yourself why you had to let them go and that they are happier now than they might have been if they'd stayed. Send love, so much love, and thanks too for all that they brought to your life.

Grieving For A Dog You Never Knew

Something that I've always found hard is reading or hearing about a dog that has been in difficult, sad or challenging circumstances, even though I never knew them. It hurts immensely if it seems the dog didn't receive the love they deserved.

I can't even watch a fiction film if I know something unhappy happens to a dog in it and we'll check the website, www.doesthedogdie.com if we're about to watch a film that has a dog in it.

If I see a headline in the news or social media that doesn't bode well about a dog often I can't bear to read it, just in case. But then it plays on my mind and I have to go back and face it, hoping that there was some happy ending.

When you're a dog lover your heart can feel the grief of any dog in distress even if you've never met. You know that, given the chance, you could have rescued that dog, given it love and a wonderful life.

But the tragedy comes when it's too late and it seems there's nothing you can do to make it right.

When something is left undone like this our minds can play it over and over but we're helpless to change what happened.

What to do

If there's anything practical you can do, like campaigning or donating, then consider that as a way of bringing something good out of their pain. Pay their life, or the loss of it, forward in some way. Take the energy of the emotions you're feeling and use it to some good. Promise them you'll do your best to help another dog in need if you can.

If you have time then volunteer at a dog shelter giving other dogs the love that they need on behalf of this dog.

Do a fundraiser to raise awareness or money in their memory. Or if you have space in your life then there are many dogs, possibly who've been through something similar, to pour the energy of your love into.

Spend some time sending that dog your love. Even though you never met them tell them you're so sorry. Imagine being with them and helping them in some way, even if it's just giving them company and comfort in their time of need. Show them that they're loved or not alone or whatever it is that they crave.

Then, whatever your own beliefs allow, see them in some way being welcomed into loving arms, having left behind the trauma of whatever happened, to talk about all they learnt and all they tried to teach.

And when they're ready to have another go, imagine them coming back here again into a new life as a puppy. This time they'll be somewhere they are completely adored and all that went on before in their previous life is now forgotten and they're living in this moment, being loved.

Any pain that you've felt on behalf of this dog is a sign you have a beautiful, big heart. And the world and dogs need more people like you.

Walk Six
Helping Others Who Are Grieving

When our dog has gone we may well not be alone in our grief.

We can, hopefully, share with other adults in our family how we're all feeling and understand each other but it can be harder to know how to help any children who are missing their dog and also work out how to comfort a fellow dog who's been left behind.

If you're wondering what's best to do shall we look at ways you can help children and dogs in their grief?

Helping Children Cope

Little Evie was three years old when the family dog, Buttons, died. They'd had such a beautiful, close relationship ever since Buttons had watched over a newborn Evie and then let her wrap her arms around him, smothering him with affectionate as she grew into a toddler.

Through Evie's eyes he was the same species as her and she honestly believed he was her brother and best friend. Wherever Buttons went Evie was with him. So when he died it seemed impossible for her parents to know how to help Evie understand that he wasn't coming back. Every day she'd ask where he was and, if she spotted a dog that looked like him, she'd get so excited, calling out "Buttons! Buttons, come here!".

A year later a new puppy came into their lives, a very different breed to Buttons, and Evie named her Splodge. Now aged four, Evie seemed to love her and was constantly having to be watched so she didn't overwhelm and smother her with the affection that Buttons had been used to.

But one day, nine months after Splodge had arrived, Evie suddenly asked her mum what foods would make a dog die. When her mum explained all the things that were dangerous to dogs, Evie, very simplistically and without malice said "Ok. I'll give those to Splodge so that Buttons can come back now".

Through her young eyes Buttons was just waiting round the corner but held back from returning because Splodge had taken his place.

When Mike had been a young boy his family had taken him from the UK to live in America and his heart had broken when they'd re-homed his dog Bob. For a while he'd worked on a secret plan to smuggle himself onto a plane, fly back to the UK and find Bob. But his plans never worked out and all he had were the photographs of him and Bob that he kept beside his bed.

Sisters, Lottie and Milly, still cried themselves to sleep most nights, months after their dog Rosie had been stolen. They didn't let their Dad know how upset they still were as they knew he blamed himself for not watching her more closely in the garden that day and never brought up her name in front of him.

They whispered about Rosie in the dark together, imagining where she was now and if they'd ever see her again.

As adults we have the experience and hopefully some wisdom to understand and cope with our dogs no longer being there. But children, whatever their ages, may well see and feel things differently. They don't have the same level of control over what happens to their dog, are more helpless and at the mercy of what their parents decide.

It might be that the adults know it's not practical to keep the dog anymore if they're divorcing, moving away, short of time or money. Or, if the dog is ill, they'll have hopefully talked to vets, tried different treatments and then arrived at the decision it's time to let them go.

Even within the same family we all have a unique relationship with our dogs and while one person seems to have reached a peaceful place someone else may still be struggling.

Whatever has happened to your dog it can be helpful to take a moment and, putting your own feelings gently to the side, observe with compassion and without judgement, each person in your family, particularly any children. How are they really?

Think about the different ages of each child and their understanding about what's happened and their relationship with your dog.

If a child is quiet or even seems happy or not showing their feelings - what's going on underneath? It may be that all is well but if you ask them how they're feeling and they say they're fine is it just because they think that's what you want to hear?

When our dog Oliver was given away we were told not to cry or show that we missed him.

The song, "Love Me Love My Dog" by Peter Shelley was in the charts when I was 9 so I used to sing along to that with all my heart when it came on the radio. Even now if I hear it it brings back that time and how it should have been.

Much the same as when a person dies, when a dog has been part of the family everyone left behind is dealing with their own feelings and the loss of that important connection. You may all feel differently - nothing is right or wrong but respecting how each person is feeling is really important.

What Can You Do?

If you're facing the decision of having your dog put to

sleep or re-homing them then, if you possibly can, include your child in your thinking using language that they'll understand, not to worry or scare them but to help them begin to understand why something is about to happen.

If it's after the event, being mindful of your child's age, gently explain to them why you had to give the dog away or why he or she died.

Give everyone space to talk about the dog if they want to. Let them know it's ok to show their feelings, whatever they are, and that some day they'll feel more happiness than sadness when they think about them.

It can be tricky for some to know what to say about heaven if they're asked. I may go against what others think here but if the main aim is to help your child and if they want to believe in heaven for pets, even if you don't, then just agree with them. Follow their lead if they give one. If they say that they think your dog is still around, even if you don't think so, then tell them they could well be right and ask them why they think that. Their answers may surprise you and even bring you some comfort. I often think children are more receptive spirituality than grown-ups are.

I remember a teacher at my school, who was a nun, being asked by a child if animals went to heaven. The nun said "No" and even back then I wondered why she'd said that. What was the good in crushing a child's hopes? And who was she to know for sure that our beloved animals won't be waiting for us? How could another being that we've shared so much love with not be part of heaven when we get there?

If your dog has gone missing then ask your children if they'd like to be involved in trying to find him or her. If they do then they could join you on search parties, help make posters or record videos to put on social media. When you're encouraging them to be as involved as they'd like to be you're giving them a sense of some control rather than helplessness.

When your dog has gone talk about them together - the best things about them, what you miss the most, what you don't miss, share funny stories and memories. Maybe make this something you do together once a week or every evening before bed.

When you're out walking hold hands together and shout out "We miss you" "We love you"

If your dog has died or been re-homed help your children decide what to do with their belongings. They may want to hold onto them or go and personally hand them to another dog. Do whatever you can that feels right for them as it will really help them know their feelings have been heard.

I'd be tempted, if your child says to throw their things away, to take those items out of the house and store them at a friend's house for a couple of weeks, letting them think you've got rid of them. If they then really regret their decision and so wish they still had the chewed up toy as a comforter, you can bring it back as a surprise.

I think often of teenagers, Arthur and Ella, and how a sad situation had been made easier for them. They'd made the choice to be with their parents when their worn out dog, Betty, was put to sleep. They'd talked through with the vet beforehand what would happen on the day and decided, however painful it was for them, they wanted Betty to know they were all there with her.

They'd gathered her favourite toys and blankets next to her and told her stories about when she was a puppy as she gently slipped away. As a family they grieved openly, talking about Betty most days, letting each other know how much they missed her.

134

Even if some time has now passed after your dog has gone it may well be worth gently checking in with your children to see how they're doing and whether they'd like to talk about your dog. Their answers may surprise you and, even if they don't want to talk now, let them know that the door is always open and you'll listen to however they're feeling.

Helping Dogs Grieve

I really believe that dogs do grieve and, as they're not able to talk things through or understand where their friend has gone, it must be very confusing. So it doesn't feel right leaving them out of this book if they too may be missing a fellow dog.

And when you're coping with your own grief your spare capacity to know how to help others, including other dogs, can be thin on the ground.

Just like humans every dog is unique and so while one of them may barely notice the sudden absence of a woolly friend another could well be pining away.

They can also pick up on our feelings and the change in the atmosphere of a home. They don't necessarily know the dog has died, just that it's not there and they may spend time searching or waiting for it to come back. This can feel distressing to the humans and be a constant, painful reminder of the loss.

Some of the things you might see in their behaviour can be signs of anxiety; Pacing, destruction, loss of appetite, aggression, lethargy. They may be more clingy, not wanting to leave your side, or even seem to be distancing themselves from you.

If you try and step inside their minds you might find some glimmers of understanding and a way forward. It's worth thinking about how their lives are now different.

~ How much did their daily routine involve the other dog?
~ Did they play or provide company for each other?
~ May they have looked to their companion as the leader of

the pack, someone to protect them, and now they're lost or afraid?

∼ Are you treating them any differently now the other one has gone?

∼ Could they be picking up on your distress and think they've done something wrong or they're sad because you're sad?

It's very easy for us to see human emotions in dogs and to think they have a similar concept of dying that we do. It's normal for us to project our grief and think they're feeling the same. This is where a bit of your own detective work is needed to try and work out what they're thinking and the emotions that are going on inside their beautiful minds.

You know your own dog better than anyone and a bit of trial and error may be needed to see what works.

Some of these ideas may sound contradictory but, as our dogs can't tell us what they're thinking, we need to work out what they need.

Things To Try

Give them extra fuss and praise if they come asking for it. They may be confused as their pack has grown smaller and need reassurance from you that they're still loved and you won't be disappearing as well.

Leave them in peace if they need it. Be mindful that you may be giving them the extra attention you would have given the other dog so they're getting a double helping. This might be wonderful for them but carefully see for just one day what happens when you give them the usual amount of fuss they had before. If it looks like they're craving more then give it freely.

Invite one of their dog friends over to play if they're sociable and missing that interaction and company.

Ask their favourite people over too as they'll bring fresh energy and a distraction.

If your dog thrives when other dogs are around it may be worth thinking about whether you're ready to introduce another one into your lives permanently.

Treat them to a new toy or game so they see that life can still be fun. In their childlike innocence something fresh and exciting can help them forget for a while that someone is missing.

Dogs are creatures of habit so keep their usual routine the same if you can - food and walks at normal times - and add in favourite or new places. If they still have the same daily structure it will help them feel secure. Bringing in new adventures alongside this will freshen up their days.

How you are feeling may well affect your dog and vice versa. It's hard trying to hold it all together when you're grieving and when we try and stop emotions they just build and become stronger.

If you need space to bawl your eyes out, and you know it would upset them, see if a friend or dog walker can take them out so you have the time and privacy you need. Or leave them at home for an hour or so and take yourself somewhere where you can let it all out in peace.

If they're waiting or searching for their friend then distract them with a game or some treats.

A new environment can be helpful, even for a couple of days, so if you're able to take a dog-friendly break away together a change of scene could do you all some good.

If you're worried, especially if they're not eating or drinking much, then a trip to the vets is a good idea. They can then give them a physical check-up and may even prescribe a pheromone product for a while to reduce stress and help calm them.

Don't be offended if your dog doesn't seem upset or even appears happier. They don't know that the other one isn't coming back shortly and may just be enjoying the peace and quiet or your undivided attention while it lasts. Remember that dogs don't hide the way they're feeling the way we do and in this very moment they may be relishing not being rough and tumbled with or having their toys stolen.

However your dog is behaving treat them as normally as possible, reinforcing the behaviour you want and gently discouraging and redirecting when needed.

Be patient and give them time to adjust. Dogs live in the present and, with patience, are capable of adapting, with happiness, to a new way of life.

Walk Seven
Getting Another Dog

Anna felt so lost. Her precious dog Stanley had died only a few weeks ago and she knew there would never be another dog like him. That connection, that love, had been unique. He'd been a challenge at the beginning when she'd rescued him and, although it was almost impossible to believe now, there had been times in their first few months together when she'd thought she'd made a terrible mistake. But she'd persevered, giving him as much patience and understanding as she could. And slowly it had begun to pay off. As the months rolled into years he grew under her care into the most faithful, loving dog. She knew for sure that there could never be the same love with another dog.

But she was so incredibly lost and the only thing that seemed to ease that feeling was looking at the pictures of dogs on the animal rehoming website, all longing for a home. She'd look for a while and then with shame and disappointment at herself close that site down and head back into her loss.

When you've felt the pain of your dog dying it can be so unbearable that the urge to fill that gaping hole is immense. We can find ourselves being helplessly drawn to ads for cute puppies or dog rescue sites where a dog seems to be pleading directly with us to take him home.

We may be filled with guilt that we're so easily thinking of replacing our dearest friend so we try and turn our minds away from all thoughts of other dogs. But the pain is so terrible and the only thing that keeps us going is the glimmer of hope when we think about bringing another dog into our lives. And then the guilt starts again.

Sometimes if we put off making a decision for long enough the urge can fade enough for us to begin to appreciate the lie-ins or being able to stay in the warm on a cold, rainy day. Money can begin to grow again in our bank accounts and spontaneous trips away are suddenly possible.

And yet, there it is. That pull towards another dog and then the confusion and dismay at ourselves that we could even be thinking that way.

When we've allowed a dog into our lives and our hearts I believe we have literally grown in our compassion, our knowledge, our love. We know what's possible because we've been there and felt it and lived it. And when it's suddenly gone we mourn for that which we had. Because we now know. Our eyes were opened and they can never un-see again that love and connection that is possible between two completely different species. We can wear glasses that obscure, choose to look the other way, but it only takes a moment, a quick glance at a dog website or the sight of a puppy walking past, and we're right back staring the love and the loss in the heart again.

So the yearning is there because we want and need to have that love again. But alongside the yearning can come the feeling that we're betraying and being unfaithful to our friend.

We also know that, if we were to get another dog, we'd be opening ourselves up to the future pain of loss all over again.

Guilt

When we feel guilt about something in the past it's impossible to go back and change what happened. We can try and make amends in some way but we can't turn back the clock.

But if you're feeling guilty about something in the present then there are ways to make that better.

It may be that you're thinking about, or are even in the process of, bringing another dog into your life but the guilt is alongside you, holding you back from enjoying the hope and excitement that are struggling to come to the surface.

Try this:

Find a place where you can be quiet for a moment.

Be still and allow the guilt in its own time to come to the front.

Say thank you to it and that you are sure it's got something important to tell you. Let it know that you'll really listen.

Without judging or arguing allow the intention of that feeling to come through. It may be that the guilt is worried your previous dog will think you've abandoned or replaced him too easily. Maybe it's concerned that once you give your love to a new dog there won't be any left for your old one.

It could be that the guilt is trying to punish you for allowing your dog to die, telling you that you could have done more and that you don't deserve another chance.

Whatever it's saying really listen and genuinely thank it as perhaps it's doing its best and the job it believes it needs to do.

Then bring in some gentle questioning. Is whatever it's saying true? Really true? So, if you do get another dog, would that mean there honestly wouldn't be any love left for your old dog? Or could it be that our hearts know how to expand so there will always be plenty to spare? Is it possible that actually having a new dog will make you love your old dog even more because he was the one who taught you about the gift of loving dogs?

If the guilt is saying you could have done more to prevent your dog from dying then again gently ask if that is really true. If it is then face it full on, say how deeply sorry you are and that you've learnt the toughest lesson and will from now on do all that you can to help any dogs in the future.

If actually you really did do all you could, or whatever you felt was best at the time, then listen to that truth. Remembering that hindsight is a wonderful thing and most of us, at some point, wish we could go back in time, knowing what we know now.

What if I forget my dog?

That's a fear many people have about bringing another dog into their lives and why also, very often it feels important to hold onto the grief and pain. When you're hurting you're not forgetting. If we're happy it can feel disloyal.

But what if you could always remember but without the pain? And even remember more when grief isn't blocking the memories?

If you imagine for a moment that you have 100% capacity to remember and think about your dog. If the pain is huge it's probably taking up say 80% of that capacity so when you think about your dog you feel sadness and loss which can become the main feelings. And only 20% is left for memories that bring you pure joy, without the hurt.

When you're able to leave some of that awful sadness behind you will free up more of that capacity to remember the things that made you laugh, the joyful love and the wonderful times you shared. It doesn't mean you won't miss them, ache for them, mourn them, but you will be free to remember them for all that they were, for their whole life with you, and not just the end and final days and the pain.

Their lives and times with us are a whole, beautiful book. When we keep re-reading just the final chapter we miss out on all that came before. And they are worth so much more than that.

Welcoming a new dog into your life will, hopefully, bring you happiness. Even though the new dog won't fit exactly into the hole left in your heart by the dog you miss, it will fill it enough to be a buffer and free up some of that capacity so you can remember them more with laughter than tears.

Try this:

Something that's very useful to do, as soon as you can after your dog dies, is to write down as many memories as

145

possible, describe their character, good and bad, their idio-syncrasies, the feel of their fur, the smell of them. Keep a note of the tricks they could do, their favourite people and dog friends, toys, the things they disliked. So that you have a written record in case you ever question yourself. Hopefully you'll have photos and videos so you can make a note of when they were taken and the kind of days they were. The idea is to capture their character and what made them so special in as much detail as you can so you won't worry that you'll ever forget.

Even if there are days or months in the future that you do think you've forgotten your dog, he or she is still living in the fibres of your heart, and that love has been woven so beauti-fully and so seamlessly that it's there without you even realising.

What if I can't love the new dog as much?

No love is exactly the same. It can't be because every one of us and every single animal we bring into our lives is unique. When we're hurting so much we're desperate to have that love back again. In our naivety we can believe and hope that we'll feel just the same about a new dog.

So off we go and fetch that puppy or the rescue dog and the shock can then hit us that we haven't got our old dog back. In many ways that can re-open the grief.

It can be crushingly disappointing when the truth settles in that your new dog isn't your old dog back in another body.

It's really normal to compare the new arrival with the friend we've lost. There may be parts of their character that, although hard to admit, you actually prefer or something you wish for in your new dog that the old one had.

Dogs are not all the same. Even if they're the same breed, colour and sex, even from the same litter, they will all be different. It's very similar to children from the same family who look different and have their own personalities. A new dog may well end up sharing some learned behaviours because of how you are with them but gently prepare yourself that this isn't your dog coming back. Not better or worse, just different. This is the chance for a unique, wonderful, new connection and love to begin to form and your heart will grow even more to include their new shape as well as the original one.

Try this:

As with any new connection, in the early days you're getting to know each other, the things you love and the bits you don't like so much. Being honest with yourself or someone you trust about how you're feeling can be very helpful.

Take the pressure off yourself and give yourself time. Relationships are all different. Sometimes it really is love at first sight but other times it takes a while to grow. If we feel forced into a feeling that's not coming naturally it can have the opposite effect. Just like if you brought a friend's child to play with yours because they were the same age and assumed they'd get on. If you're lucky it might work but trying to push them to like each other the first time could halt what may have become a lovely friendship in its tracks.

If you're doing all you can and the bond just isn't forming then, if it's possible and you have someone to care for them, have a break for a few days away from each other. Absence really can make the heart grow fonder and experiencing the greeting you'll get once you meet again can begin to melt enough of your heart to allow them in. You may also have found yourself missing or worrying about them while you're apart and this can be a sign of a relationship forming.

But if you're just relieved when they're not there and your heart sinks when you see them again, it can be hard to face but maybe you aren't right for each other. If you think this could possibly be the case then give it another chance to see what happens while you tentatively find out if their breeder or the re-homing centre will take them back.

Keeping your dog's best interests at heart, once you've given it enough of an opportunity for love to start growing and it just isn't, then the kindest thing may be to find a new home for them before they become too attached to you and there are lots of broken hearts. Somewhere there will be a family where the chemistry is right and they will find their fit in a forever home.

To wait or not?

I wonder if there ever is the perfect time to bring a new dog into our lives when we've lost the one we loved?

In the early days of grief our minds can be overwhelmed with emotion and it's hard to think rationally. Giving yourself a bit of space to gather your thoughts may feel so hard but if you can just take it one day at a time and tell yourself you'll think about looking for a new dog tomorrow or maybe next week. Do that day by day, checking in with yourself to see how you're feeling, taking the pressure off but still keeping hope alive.

Sometimes, even if we've told ourselves we'll wait, a new

dog will find us. Or it may be that, even if you keep looking, that special dog hasn't appeared just yet.

But whatever happens, if you allow some quiet and calmness into your heart and trust that the right thing will come about then you'll be in the best state possible when it does.

Try this:

Take a moment when it's safe to close your eyes and imagine you're standing at a Crossroads.

One path is the Decision To Wait A While before finding another dog.

The other path is to Find One As Soon As Possible.

Neither path is right or wrong. You're going to imagine going along each path for the next six months to see how you feel. Take as much time as you need to really get a sense of what it's like following each decision. Notice how you're feeling, what's changed in your life, the good and the not so good parts of each choice.

Take a few calm breaths, letting the out breath be longer than the in breath, to calm your mind.

Then step along the path of the Decision To Wait A While.

Imagine you've just decided that you'll give it six months before you start looking. How does that feel?

Keep going along that path as you imagine you're a couple of weeks further forward, then a month, then three months, then six.

For each time check in with yourself and see how you're feeling. Keep asking yourself was that a good decision you made back at the start of the path to wait?

When you get to six months time are you ready to start

looking for another dog now or would you like to wait a while longer?

From this point along that path at six months in the future ask your Wisdom Self to give a message to the you back here in the present time.

Bring yourself back to the Crossroads. Take some more calm breaths and then, when you're ready, begin along the path to Find One As Soon As Possible.

Imagine you've decided today is the day to begin your search for a dog. How does that feel?

Keep going along this path as you imagine you're a couple of weeks further forward in your quest, then a month, then three months, then six.

So somewhere in this time frame see yourself finding your new dog.

From the moment of your first decision to then bringing this dog home keep checking in with yourself and see how you're feeling. Keep asking yourself was that a good choice you made back at the start of the path to find one as soon as possible?

When you get to six months time notice if you think it was the right decision. From this point along that path at six months in the future ask your Wisdom Self to give a message to the you back here in the present time.

Bring yourself back to the Crossroads, take a few more calm breaths and open your eyes again.

Carrying The Love On

Whatever you decide to do the dog you've lost would want you to carry their love on in whatever way feels right for you.

If you have to quickly find another to fill that hole, or if you can't bear the thought of opening your heart again, both show how much you miss them.

The love to and from your dog will carry on whatever choice you make.

And remember, through their eyes you can do no wrong.

Walk Eight
From This Moment On

The times we've shared with our dog, maybe without even realising it, have enriched our lives and deepened our wisdom. When we look into our hearts we may begin to see how dogs have shown us how to be better people.

We have the chance to remember and keep with us all they've shown us, to let their wonderfulness live on through us and never be forgotten, from this moment and for always.

Dogs Are Our Teachers

The best kind of lessons are those that carry on long after our teacher has gone. They inspire us by example and find ways to bring out the best in us.

And dogs, I believe, are some of the most wonderful teachers we'll ever have the privilege of knowing. They see the potential in us that we had no idea even existed.

This book would never have come to life if my own eyes and heart hadn't been opened by our dog, Poppy, and she truly is the inspiration behind it.

If we take a moment and see what dogs are showing us, capture the joy and look at life through their eyes, we have an amazing opportunity to grow.

All that they've taught us, if we allow it, can help us be better people, more loving and open not only with dogs but with people too.

In our grief let's remember our teachers and let their lessons live on through us.

Through the heartache pause in remembrance and gratitude for what we know now, and so much more, with thanks to our friends, our wonderful, glorious dogs...

Unconditional love

How incredible to have experienced what this feels like, to be loved no matter what we look like, what jobs we have, how much money's in our accounts, or how successful we are.

When you know your dog loves you just as much when you wake up dishevelled in the morning as when you're all dressed up, when their faces light up every time you walk through the door, when they couldn't care less if you earn your money by scrubbing floors or being a national celebrity, that has been one of the most profound lessons on receiving unconditional love. To not be judged.

And when you've loved a dog and know that you may well dive into freezing water to save them or let them breathe on you with doggy breath or get up in the middle of the night if they need a wee or love them with tenderness when they're old and frail, you too have shown them that unconditional love. And, even if you haven't realised it, you've proved to yourself who you truly are.

We can carry that lesson on, long after our dogs have gone, and try our best to give and receive that sort of love with other people and animals that come into our lives.

To see the best in ourselves

So often in life we are far more unkind to ourselves than we would be to someone else. We're negative, harsh, focusing on our faults and the things we did wrong.

But dogs hold up a magical mirror to us that shows just the best bits, the way that they see us. Even when we've done something wrong, accidentally trodden on their tail or scolded them, they can look at us with astonishment that this isn't who we really are and they're either momentarily taken by surprise or think it must have been their fault.

They see the wonderfulness in us and believe in our potential. And so we may just find ourselves trying to live up to the identity that they've given us.

There are some wonderful quotes and even some songs that sum it up, just like "Make Me The Man My Dog Thinks I Am" by Jimmy Scott.

But once our greatest fan and cheerleader has left us though who are we now? Maybe, just possibly, whisper it to yourself, you do have all those wonderful bits about you and when you take the mask of insecurities away you might just be able to glimpse yourself as your dog saw you.

The lesson here, according to our dogs, is to love and accept ourselves in our purest form, to try to do and be our best whilst knowing that we're adorable just the way we are.

To be in the moment

As human beings we're often so busy rushing here and there, trying to get somewhere or something done, that it takes a two week holiday for us to stop. And then we can often feel guilty that we're not achieving enough or the act of stopping brings on that cold or bug our body's been keeping at bay.

Dogs, however, when left to their own pace and not being rushed along by us, seem to have it right. When they see something that excites them they race towards it, if there's a patch of grass with an interesting smell they'll spend as long as they need analysing every blade and picking up their messages. If they're tired they'll take a nap, when the roast chicken's taken out of the oven they're immediately there to help. They could have had a long car journey stuck in traffic but as soon as the car pulls into the carpark and they sniff the sea all that's forgotten and they're racing down to the beach as soon as the door has opened.

A dog will find the wonder wherever they are. An old, shabby caravan is just as interesting as a palace to them and while we're often looking for the next best thing we can miss the beauty in each very fleeting moment.

Dogs seem to have embraced the Japanese word "arama-hoshi", the art of enjoying small pleasures and not craving more.

They are the most wonderful inspirers of how to live in the present and in our hectic lives it would do us so much good, whenever we can, to be more like our dogs in this way.

Every now and then pause for a moment and notice the beauty in everyday things.

Instead of thinking ahead to all you need to get done or what's happening later, take a few calm breaths and focus on something in front of you. Maybe it's the shape of a leaf on a pot plant or the warmth of your hands on a radiator, the chimneys standing proud on roofs, tiny flowers growing amongst the blades of grass, the pattern of the cracks in the pavement.

Don't let it pass you by this time but see it, smell it, feel it. Let your dog's lesson in the joy of life bring light to the ordinary.

To forgive and not hold grudges

Wouldn't life be easier if we had the ability that dogs do to let go of things so quickly?

Unless they're being treated consistently badly, within a few moments of being told off or denied a share of our meal, it's in the past, left behind and forgotten.

They don't hold it against us or bring it up in years to come. There are no weapons being stored or hurtful memories to wound us when they feel like it.

Imagine if we could embrace our dogs' ability to forgive so easily? To say "That really hurt me" and then, like magic, it's gone? To turn our world into a place without grudges, resentments and hurt but peaceful harmony with compassion rather than judgement instead.

To be loyal and faithful

However much fun a dog is having at a friend's house if you grab your coat and keys as if to leave the chances are they'll be right there by your side, making sure you don't forget them. Dogs have immense loyalty and, once you've developed a connection, it's yours for safe keeping.

They can be complete tarts, giving their attention to someone with treats in their pocket, but they've still got one eye on your movements.

They'll follow you walking through a rainy night if needed, stay by your side if you fall and hurt yourself, defend you from an attacker and lay beside you when you're not well.

In their eyes you're always right and, unlike a human friend, they'll unquestionably stick up for you whatever you've said or done.

So how may we continue this lesson in faithful loyalty on their behalf? Somehow it seems much harder for us to show this to people than it is for our dogs. But if we try and see the person as their dog would see them, look for their best intentions, give them the benefit of the doubt where possible then we'll be part of the way there. If we can, for just a moment, be on their side instead of against them then we may see things through their eyes. And even if we'd like them to behave differently, it's far easier to show them how to do this as a friend rather than an enemy.

To show our emotions

The expression "Wear your heart on your sleeve" must surely have been created about dogs.

Imagine a world where you go for supper at a friend's house, you sniff the plate of food they've given you, don't fancy it and just walk away.

Or you pass a table of strangers eating their pub lunch, grab someone's steak and stuff it in your mouth.

As your partner arrives home from work you run around the house, jumping on and off the sofa and chairs with excitement.

Maybe you meet a stranger in the street, don't like the look of them, and shout abuse in their face, or fall instantly in love with them and want a rough and tumble game right there and then.

Their emotions are pure, unhidden, simple and uninhibited. They have such freedom, if we allow it, to be exactly who they are.

Unless we've tried to train it out of them, when a dog is happy it wags its tail, jumps up, runs around and grabs its toys as gifts. It doesn't stop for a moment to try and hide its joy.

Likewise when it's sad or bored, angry or scared, you know about it. In many ways a dog is like a child before they've learnt social etiquette or how to contain their feelings. Maybe that's why there often seems to be a connection and an understanding between dogs and young children.

Dogs don't seem to have the same level of subtlety or complication that humans have with showing how they feel.

Their emotions are pure and uncensored and you can easily tell what they're thinking and feeling. You don't have to guess or wonder if you've upset them or whether they like you. And this can be hugely refreshing and rewarding. A friendship with a dog is about the most uncomplicated relationship you will ever get. No second guessing, no doubting. Just pure, undiluted emotion.

No wonder then that when we lose our friend it cuts so deep.

Maybe dogs are here to teach us to be more open with our own feelings, to not hold back when we love someone, to be unashamed to say if we're afraid and to be free, literally, to jump with joy.

Gratitude

Our dog Poppy will watch me spooning yoghurt out of the pot and into my mouth, her eyes carefully following the spoon's journey. Once I've scraped out nearly all of the yoghurt I'll then give her the pot to lick. It then becomes her new, brilliant treasure and she'll carry it off to a private place to get every last tiny taste out of it.

It continues to amaze me that she's just watched me eating mouthful after mouthful and yet is delighted with the scrapings that are left for her to lick. If she'd been a person waiting for her turn she would probably be outraged at the unfairness of her share.

And yet a quick stroke on their heads, a crumb dropped on the floor, a kind word and they're happy.

It's not that they have low expectations or opinions of themselves but just seem to naturally practice gratitude.

What would our lives be like if we could do the same? There have been many studies on what happens when we focus on the things in our lives to be grateful for and this doesn't mean being overly positive or pretending nothing's wrong but seeing the good or what we've learnt from negative situations. Where our thoughts go our feelings follow.

While I'm writing this I have a broken ankle and torn ligaments after I fell over in the same field where I tripped and broke my wrist last year. It's far from ideal and I have been thinking of taking up extreme sports rather than dog walking.

But I have a choice. I can feel sorry for myself. Or I can look at it a bit differently. I can acknowledge that it's painful and really inconvenient being unable to drive for six weeks and yet I was so lucky not to break my ankle and wrist at the same time. I have the most wonderful partner looking after me and friends offering to walk our dog and help if needed and a house filled with beautiful flowers and gifts that people have sent.

What we focus on we get more of and dogs focus on the delight of the dropped crumbs or nearly empty yoghurt pot rather than the full human meal they've just missed out on. So, rather than being disappointed, they're filled with happiness instead.

This doesn't mean lowering our own expectations but noticing the wonderful things too, however small they are.

Care for and nurture another being

There's a beautiful Hawaiian word, Kahu, which means an honoured attendant, guardian, nurse, caretaker or protector. And if you've cared for a dog you too have been a Kahu. They haven't been your property, you never really owned them, but instead you were entrusted with the safekeeping of a precious soul during their time with you.

I remember very early on in the days of our Poppy being a puppy learning how often we'd need to say no to invitations if we'd be away too long, always putting her welfare first, being her guardians and protectors.

It can be even more obvious if you have no children to care for as suddenly you become a parent to another being who will never become independent of you.

And our dogs have taught us that we're capable of that care, and have shown us we can put another's needs very often before our own. It can be a tough class to take but the feeling when you know you've done it right should be one of immense pride.

To carry that teaching on there will always be a plentiful supply of people and animals in need of your care. If you feel able to nurture another in the name of your dog then that would be wonderful.

But most importantly perhaps the lesson should also be about looking after ourselves as well. It's very normal to put ourselves last and this can be a time to look gently and with love at what care you need and what's possible. That after all the months or years of looking after your dog maybe this is the time to think about you for a while?

To cross boundaries

Dogs are wonderful levellers, seeing all of us as equals no matter what our class, race, education or wealth. And when you find yourself on dog walks chatting to someone who wouldn't normally be in your social circle you've already followed your dog's lead.

Having something so special in common is like a secret, unspoken language. You know the other person with their woolly friend understands, without saying a word, all that it means to love a dog. Social divides no longer matter as dogs from social housing play with those from the the grand ones. Again, like children, they haven't been indoctrinated into "differences'. They either like you or they don't and it has nothing to do with your background or status.

Friendships can be struck up between people who may never normally have crossed paths, simply because they share an understanding and love. And dogs show us that's what really matters.

We have the chance, long after our friend has gone, to see past the social constructs to the person inside. And, continuing the teachings of our dogs, we can like them or we don't have to but it needs have nothing to do with the trappings or lack of surrounding them.

Remember to laugh and play

Through the years their games may change, from the crazy energy of a puppy racing around, to the ball of an older dog, held firmly in their mouth, challenging you to win it. But their sense of fun and the love of play continues way into their adulthood.

As humans we can forget or think it's uncool to play games or we're just too busy being sensible grown-ups. Dogs though stay childlike, finding the fun where we didn't even realise it existed.

I have to hold my hand up here and admit I do still love to play and the game of a group of us quickly hiding when someone leaves the room fills me with childish delight.

When we're living with a dog we have the perfect excuse and encouragement to throw a ball, chase around, play tug and rough and tumble. We have the permission to be children again.

I remember a friend telling us, just before we picked up Poppy as a puppy, that we'd find ourselves laughing every day because of her. And it's been completely true. I have no idea if dogs understand what natural clowns they are but there's something so gorgeously funny about them.

The hole they leave behind is one of little laughter, empty and dry of fun and the contrast can feel so cold and stark.

But they've taught us so much and the best teachers love it when we remember what they've shown and the life they've opened up for us. In the early days after they've left even a smile can feel so hard to make but as time goes on, if laughter starts to cautiously creep in, welcome it with open arms. If there's fun to be had, on behalf of your dog and with thanks to them for showing you the way, take it.

I could honestly carry on and make a whole book just about the things that dogs teach us.

The way they encourage us to take the risk and open our hearts knowing the price we'll pay when we lose them; the incredible ability to communicate with another species; to have complete trust from another being; to give and receive attention. Maybe more than anything they show us what it's like to feel important, worthwhile and the centre of another's world.

May their wonderful teachings stay with us in some way, enriching us for the rest of our lives.

Walk Nine
The Love Carries On

This I know for sure. If you were handed to me again as a puppy, even knowing the pain that would come at the end because of loving you, I would still welcome you with open arms and the happiest of hearts.

The most wonderful things in life are to love and be loved, to feel wanted and needed.

Humans have frailties, tender places that are so easy for us to wound, histories that we bring to our relationships and insecurities that make us fragile. Our human relationships can be brilliant but are complicated and it doesn't take much for them to go wrong.

Dogs are pure, wearing their hearts on their sleeves, and you know where you are with them. You don't have to wonder or second guess how they're feeling, whether they like you or you've offended them. And we are more than enough for them just as we are. This builds the deepest trust in each other and the freedom to relax into one of the most beautiful connections you're ever likely to experience.

And that love you shared during their lives didn't pause during the times when you were apart. When you were busy doing something else they were somewhere in your mind. And they never forgot how much they loved you, even if you'd just disappeared to put the bins out.

That relationship has been woven into your very being. We're influenced and changed, even just in subtle ways, by those we share our lives with and dogs allow us to be ourselves, whole and true.

Real love and those deep bonds continue into a future when we're no longer together. We don't forget what we've shared and our dog stays imprinted into how we see the world, our hearts keeping hold of the shape of them forever.

Whatever the religious or spiritual beliefs you hold, the memories, the love and impact of that connection continue into the years ahead. How could that love they felt for you just disappear once they've physically gone? Somehow it's out there still, even if it is just by allowing ourselves to believe that love is so much more than us, an incredible energy in its own right, and can't be extinguished once it's been created.

What to do now to feel the love carrying on

~ Find ways to honour that love and receive it still. This could be as simple as stopping for a moment and knowing you were and will always be loved by your friend and that you loved them so much that it hurts right now. You learnt and are now a Master or Mistress of love, with all the deepest lows and the highest highs.

~ Know that you are bearing the pain of your separation instead of them. They would have found it distressing and not understood if you'd gone first. Love is often about carrying a heavy load for the other so they can run free. Maybe there were times you carried a full bottle of water in case they needed a drink or a towel to dry them after a swim. And now you're taking this weight of grief instead of them.

~ Notice how you've been shaped by having them in your life. Maybe it's that you have a bigger heart now because it's been expanded by them. Are you kinder to other animals? Do you have more compassion towards others who've lost a dog? Do you find joy in the simple things in life and find yourself more in the moment? Do you see a fallen stick or a sparkling stream that you may not have really seen before and think "They would have loved that?"

~ Dogs are good judges of character and they also don't believe in modesty. They saw you, really saw you and knew you without the mask or pretence we sometimes use with human relationships. Is there a way you can now know and accept, deep in your heart, that you were and always will be more than enough because they saw the real, raw you and adored you?

~ Imagine them by your side now, your cheerleader, encouraging you to believe in yourself, telling you their love is always there. If you begin, ever, to doubt yourself picture your dog doing whatever the challenging thing is first and then looking back at you as if to say "What are you waiting for? You can do it too. I know you can."

~ Allow a smile to warm your heart as you realise something incredibly special. You understand the pain that comes and you know that the years with a dog fly by. And still, knowing that, if you could rewind back to the day you first met your dog, with the decision to walk away or take them home, what would you do? I'm guessing most people would most probably do it all again.

Despite the incredible heartache when it ends, sharing the life of a dog is so wonderfully worth it.

Never The End

One day, when the time is right, you will be there, tail wagging at full speed, running to meet me. And there we'll be, back where we belong again by each other's sides, on our new, wonderful adventures.

There can be no end to the love for or from our dogs. Whether they're living on in our memories and stories or planting the seed of another dog needing to be with us, that connection will always be there.

Once you've really loved a dog you'll have learnt another language that you will never forget.

Your heart will have grown and your eyes opened to a simpler view of life that involves joy, loyalty and deep, loving connections.

When a heart has grown in this way, changed to include the shape of a dog, it can never go back to how it was before. That dog-shaped part will still be there. Always. And that's why it hurts so much. And that's why, if we breathe in some peace and quieten our minds, we may just see that it is actually an honour to carry that pain because we would never have felt it if our hearts hadn't grown in this way.

To all the dogs who we have loved, to all those we grieve and long for, we miss you so much.

For all the lessons that you taught us and the better people you believed us to be we thank you and will love and remember you always.

One day, somewhere over a rainbow bridge, with a deeper joy than we've ever known, we'll be together again.

The End?
Never.

Walk Ten
Other Resources

If you need to talk to someone:

Blue Cross - Pet Bereavement
Helping you cope with the loss of a pet, either through death, enforced separation or theft. The Pet Loss Support team is there when joy turns to sadness.
You can call 0800 096 6606.
The helpline is available between 8.30am and 8.30pm every day.
Search for 'Blue Cross pet bereavement'

The Ralph Site
A not-for-profit website that provides support to pet carers — offers help to those who are struggling with the loss of a pet. The site is dedicated to all the animals that have touched and continue to touch the hearts of so many people.
Head over to their website and you will find advice on dealing with grief, ideas for ways to memorialise your furry

friend, pet bereavement counsellors/support training, and quotes and poems to lift you up when you are sad.
Search for 'Pet loss support The Ralph Site'

Living with Pet Bereavement
The team at Living With Pet Bereavement offer free support to those who are dealing with the loss of a pet. You can either choose to have a phone call or a virtual Zoom call (additional fees) with an expert. Simply book a support session online and you will be appointed a Pet Bereavement Counsellor who will support you through the grieving process.
Search for 'Living with pet bereavement'

The Ease Animal Charity
EASE understands the importance and death of a human/pet relationship, providing plenty of helpful free resources to help those suffering. Some of the services they offer include podcasts to offer comfort and support, additional support sheets on topics such as preparing for pet loss, and a helpful guide on coping with pet bereavement in children.
Search for 'The Ease animal charity'

Help if you're struggling financially or with time to care for your dog:

Dogs Trust
A charity helping dogs in need and owners who need advice or a helping hand.
As part of their care they run these wonderful projects:

Hope Project - helping people and their dogs stay together if they're homeless or in a housing crisis
Freedom Project - provides free and confidential temporary foster care for dogs, enabling owners fleeing domestic abuse to access a refuge without the fear of what may happen to their dog if left behind.
Search for 'Dogs' Trust'.

PDSA
A charity offering people receiving certain benefits low-cost or free healthcare for their animals in the UK.
Search for 'PDSA'

Borrow My Doggy
Free help from dog lovers who can walk and care for your dog.
Search for 'Borrow my doggy'

Help if your dog has gone missing:

Battersea
Battersea's Lost Dogs and Cats Line is open seven days a week from 8am - 5pm to receive reports of missing or found animals within the M25 area. Call 020 7627 9245
Search for 'lost dogs Battersea'.

Dog Lost
Reunites lost, stray and stolen dogs with their owners.
Search for 'dog lost'.

Drone to Home
Lost dog search and rescue charity that uses drones to find lost pets.
Search for 'Drone to home'.

DroneSAR
A volunteer service helping to locate and reunite lost dogs with their owners across the UK.
Search for 'DroneSAR'.

Things I've talked about in my book:

Search 'Dream lecture - Joe Griffin'
Search 'Emotional Freedom Technique'
Search 'Human Givens Institute'

About the Author

Pippa Shay has worked as a psychotherapist and grief counsellor for over eighteen years, often with clients who are grieving over their dog who's died.

Pippa trained in Solution-focused psychotherapy based on teachings from the Human Givens Institute where she leant about the importance of meeting our emotional basic needs. These have proved to be a breakthrough with helping clients and the key discovery in why our dogs mean so much to us and why it's devastating when they die.

In a previous life Pippa was a BBC radio presenter and producer. She now often combines the two careers and gives radio and television interviews on a wide range of well-being subjects.

Most importantly she's a dog lover and her woolly friend, Poppy, has been the inspiration behind "*Not Just A Dog*".

Printed in Dunstable, United Kingdom